REDUCING PROJECT RISK

Reducing Project Risk

RALPH L KLIEM
IRWIN S LUDIN

Gower

Published by
Gower Publishing Limited
Gower House
Croft Road
Aldershot
Hampshire GU11 3HR
England

Gower
Old Post Road
Brookfield
Vermont 05036
USA

British Library Cataloguing in Publication Data

Kliem, Ralph L.
    Reducing project risk
    1. Industrial project management   2. Risk management
    I. Title   II. Ludin, Irwin S.
    658.4'04

ISBN 0 566 07799 X

Library of Congress Cataloging-in-Publication Data

Kliem. Ralph L.
    Reducing project risk / Ralph L. Kliem and Irwin S. Ludin.
        p.   cm.
    Includes index.
    ISBN 0–566–07799–X (cloth)
    1. Risk management.   I. Ludin, Irwin S.   II. Title
HD61.K595   1997
658.15'5—dc21
                                                                96–37780
                                                                CIP

Typeset in Palatino by Manton Typesetters, 5–7 Eastfield Road, Louth, Lincolnshire,
UK and printed in Great Britain by Hartnoll Limited, Bodmin.

To

Aunt Hen and Uncle Herb Orrison – RLK

My Very Special Daughter Melissa – ISL

Contents

Figures

Preface

For most companies, embarking on a project involves investing people, equipment, supplies, time, and effort. Such investment translates into money. If the project 'fails' it is a lost investment. And no company can sustain too many project failures and remain in business or be profitable for very long, regardless of industry.

But how do companies and organizations know if they have accounted for the major risks facing their projects? How do they know whether they have the right project management disciplines in place to manage those risks? How do they know if they will achieve the most important goals with the right disciplines in place?

Commonality

Most companies don't know. That's why so many of them experience the common problems of excessive costs, inadequate schedule performance, poor quality, and unmotivated people. According to a survey by the Center for Project Management, fewer than 25 per cent of US companies implement thorough, complete project management processes.[1]

Here are some more sobering statistics on the fate of different projects in different industries.

Client/server (C/S) projects develop distributed information systems that run some programs and data on a microcomputer and others on a larger computer (for example, a minicomputer). These projects cost more than expected, the schedule slips dramatically, and the result is a product that often leaves just about everyone dissatisfied. The Standish Group International Inc. found that 53 per cent of all software development projects exceed their budget and fail to complete on time.[2] The IBM Consulting Group revealed that 68 per cent of all C/S applications took too long to implement and that 55 per cent cost more than anticipated.[3]

Business process re-engineering (BPR) projects, too, have produced some sobering statistics. These projects identify better processes for accomplishing company goals. Two surveys of Fortune 1000 firms by Arthur D. Little, Inc. revealed that over 80 per cent of executives expressed dissatisfaction with BPR efforts and over 65 per cent of information systems had 'unanticipated' or 'unintended' side effects.[4]

Even Hollywood has had less than stellar statistics on project performance. *Waterworld* was costly with movie professionals comparing it to other disasters, such as *Ishtar* and *Heaven's Gate*. Other well-known movies have had less than stellar project results, including *Terminator 2* (which exceeded its budget by US $10 million); *Alien 3* (which was a year late); and *Die Hard 2* (which was US $20 million over budget).[5] It seems that even the movie business, with all its heroes, could not stop risks from having a costly impact.

Different views

Most risk management efforts concentrate only on a project's financial goals and impacts. Although important, project goals and impacts are frequently more than financial. Many movies exceed their budget but Hollywood moguls consider them a success based upon other goals or criteria. The US Space Program, especially the space shuttle, has not been a financial success yet it has achieved much of importance when viewed from the perspective of astro-physicists. If financial goals were the sole goal of projects a *Cleopatra* movie or a space shuttle programme might never have existed.

The success of a project depends on the results it is supposed to achieve. But achieving results successfully depends on how well companies manage the risks that confront their projects. Many, however, implement projects with only a vague idea of what goals to achieve and their priority. Nor do many companies have any good idea of how well they implemented project management processes to achieve goals and even the relative importance of processes employed.

It is not surprising, therefore, to see projects having a high fatality rate or achieving poor results. However, such results need not be the norm. Ways exist to minimize risks and project managers don't need to perform elaborate mathematical calculations, use exotic software or hire a PhD in statistics.

The old English proverb, 'Hope for the best but prepare for the worst' makes sense in an environment where the chances of project failure are increasing. Of course, the best way to prepare against those odds is to implement every project management process. But that's unrealistic and few projects do, in fact, implement all the processes – which is acceptable – or put every project management discipline in place. The ideal should be to institute the right process at the right time so that the risks causing failure are minimal and odds for success high.

Fear is the common thread of why risk management is important. Everyone fears the unknown to some degree. No one knows what the future might bring or what the impact of changes will be. But project managers can prepare themselves to manage the future.

Appropriate processes

To achieve project goals efficiently and effectively risk management must be in place to identify and institute the most appropriate project management processes. A risk management approach is necessary, therefore, that is simple, quick to apply, and consistently reliable to any given environment or industry. It should offer these benefits:

- Pinpoints the priorities, strengths, and weaknesses of existing projects and the priorities of new ones
- Focuses on implementing or improving project management processes
- Provides an objective review of the 'as is' condition of a project
- Identifies 'warning' signals before it's too late
- Helps to avoid repeating weaknesses on future projects

To achieve these benefits is our purpose in writing this book. We present risk management in a manner that combines a concept with practice. Part I is an introduction to risk management and the factors that influence its success or failure. Part II defines the basics for identifying, assessing, controlling, and reporting risks. Part III is a practical example of how to apply many of the concepts and techniques covered in Parts I and II. Part IV discusses trends that will affect risk management in the future. In the appendices we present five steps for identifying risks; provide insights for selecting risk management software and an overview of the popular packages in the market; and describe a matrix suggesting ways to manage certain risks.

So, take a calculated risk and join us to learn how to manage projects successfully without the fear of the unknown.

Ralph L. Kliem
Irwin S. Ludin

Part I
Introduction to Risk Management

1 An Overview

A good understanding of risk and what it entails should be our first priority before we examine the subject in more detail.

About risk

Risk is the occurrence of an event that has consequences for, or impacts on, projects. An outcome might be poor timing of product delivery because the market window of opportunity had already closed. Differences in cultures are represented by wealth, health, leisure time, and survival. Affluent nations are considered more sophisticated than poor under-developed nations. The risk of succumbing to disease due to lack of proper medical attention is higher in Amazonia than it is in London. Moral risks may involve fidelity issues with loose morals resulting in divorce for couples who appear to be happily married. Political risks include stepping outside restricted boundaries: an outcome could be not being endorsed by the party you think is supporting you. Not being accepted by your peers for whom you are is a social risk with loneliness being an outcome. In

3

terrifying situations many people ask the question, 'Why is this happening to *me*?' More specifically, in companies and organizations, ill-defined schedules represent an economic risk that can occur on a project (see Figure 1.1 for a summary of generic risks).

Types	**Expected Outcomes**
Cultural	Poor quality of life
Economic	Financial gains/losses
Moral	Family break-up
Political	Not getting re-elected
Social	Ostracism
Spiritual	Loss of faith

Fig 1.1   A summary of generic risks

There are many ways to categorize risks.

- Acceptable vs. non-acceptable risks
- Short-term vs. long-term risks
- Positive vs. negative risks
- Manageable vs. non-manageable risks
- Internal vs. external risks

Acceptable vs. non-acceptable risks
Acceptable risks are tolerable if they occur and will not stop the project. For example, something occurs that impacts on tasks not on the critical path. Non-acceptable risks are 'show stoppers' such as something happening that slows or stops tasks on the critical path.

Short-term vs. long-term risks
Short-term risks are risks having an immediate impact and their effect may be decisive. For example, a project participant departs before completing a non-critical task. Long-term risks are

risks occurring in the distant future. They, too, may have a decisive impact; for example, the departure of an indispensable employee who has not completed his or her tasks.

Positive vs. negative risks
A risk may help or hinder a project. A positive risk, for example, is where a schedule for a non-critical activity slips in such a way that it actually benefits the completion of a critical activity; the project manager shifts resources to the critical activity without it affecting deliverables.

Manageable vs. non-manageable risks
Project managers may or may not handle a risk, either by design or by some external force. An example of a non-manageable risk is senior management arbitrarily reducing funds for a project.

Internal vs. external risks
Internal risks are unique to a project and not caused by something outside the project boundaries. An example is a task completion date slipping because the person responsible for its completion lacks the necessary skills. External risks are risks over which the project has no control. An example is senior management deciding to scale back the product to build.

Elements of risk

Regardless of how risks are categorized, project managers have five key elements to consider.

1. The probability of the occurrence of a risk. Is the probability low, medium, or high? What are the 'odds', or probability, of its occurrence, being anywhere from 0 to 100 per cent? For example, does the probability of poor scheduling occurring have a 60 per cent chance of happening? Or is the figure 75 per cent? And so on.
2. The frequency of occurrence of a risk. How often might the

event occur? For example, how many times might a project
incur slippage of an important milestone?

3.   The impact of an occurrence of a risk. What consequence
will it have? For example, will poor scheduling greatly hinder
achieving a goal or will it have a minor impact? In other
words, will it be a 'show stopper'? (See Figure 1.2 for potential areas impacted by common risks.)

● Accidents ● Financial gains/losses ● Spoilage ● Status gains/losses ● Time off from work ● Timing (good and poor)

Fig 1.2   Potential areas impacted by common risks

4.   The importance relative to other risks. For example, are
inadequate schedules more important than poor account-
ability for task completion? Not all risks are equal; some
have greater importance than others to a project's outcome.
For example, a risk may have a high probability of occurrence and a low impact. The inverse can occur where a risk
may have a low probability of occurrence and a high impact.

5.   The exposure, or vulnerability, which is the impact of a risk
on a product, system, or project. A risk can have different
levels of exposures as well as varying probabilities of occurrence based on given circumstances. Therefore, exposure is
simply the level of impact times the probability of occurrence.

To demonstrate how these five key elements relate, the following milestone shows slippage on the critical path of a delivery
schedule.

1st element is probability of slippage	40 per cent (or 0.40)
2nd element is frequency of slippage	1 time
3rd element is impact of slippage	5 (where 1 is low and 5 is high impact)
4th element is importance relative to other risks	4 (where 1 is low and 5 is high degree of importance)
5th element is vulnerability or exposure (i.e., impact × probability of occurrence)	2 ($5 \times 0.40 = 2$) [where maximum exposure is 5×100 per cent $= 5$; minimum is $1 \times 0.40 = 0.10$]

This milestone describes slippage in a delivery schedule for a security software application to a third party distributor by a specific date; additional 'spin-off' products will result from this package. An analysis indicates that the chance of slippage is 40 per cent and with a single occurrence. However, the impact is very high because the spin-offs in the queue would also slip. The relative importance of the security software versus other products is high due to the usefulness, interest, and practicality of the topic. The vulnerability, however, is that similar products could also enter and saturate the market-place. Thus, the software development firm must decide what risk management action to take.

Risk management steps

Probability, frequency, impact, importance, and exposure are the necessary factors in analysing the four vital steps in risk management. These steps are: risk identification; risk analysis; risk control; and risk reporting.

Risk identification

Considerable effort occurs in identifying and ranking the processes, or components, of a project, its major goals, and its risks.

This identification step is closely allied with the next step, risk analysis. To be effective, risk identification requires considerable up-front planning and research. Project managers need to determine the analysis technique to use; select the primary participants who are to perform the risk identification; allow participants time to perform it; and decide where to conduct it. For research, they must review project plans, interview people, calculate statistics and metrics; and peruse technical documentation.

Risk analysis

Project managers convert data collected during the risk identification step into information using a selected technique. Two categories of risk analysis exist: quantitative and qualitative. Quantitative techniques rely heavily on statistical approaches, such as the Monte Carlo simulation. Qualitative techniques rely more on judgement than on statistical calculations, such as heuristics.

Risk control

Project managers identify the measures, or controls to establish, to lessen or avoid the impact of a risk on a process or component. Project managers can take one of two approaches towards risk. They can react to risk: that is, wait for it to occur before taking any action – for example, they hire more people at the last minute. Or, they can be proactive: that is, establish plans and an infrastructure – for example, they set up an early warning system, to prepare their projects to detect and handle expected risks.

Risk reporting

Once project managers complete their identification and ranking, analysis, and control activities, they are ready to report the results. This reporting can occur as a formal presentation or as a document. Regardless, good communications skills are essential as discussing risks is sometimes a volatile topic. Heated discussions can take place over judgements made during the identification and analysis steps and about the impact of risks on a component or goal.

Risk management cycle

Project managers are mistaken if they believe that risk management is a linear process. The reality is that it is a continuous loop (see Figure 1.3). Risk identification, analysis, control, and reporting occur throughout a project. As a project proceeds through its life cycle, the more accurate and reliable risk management becomes. In other words, the level of uncertainty and ambiguity begins to decline.

To perform risk management, project managers must understand what is (might be) happening and where. We can apply the famous Deming Wheel, named after W. Edwards Deming, and use the plan, do, check, act cycle with risk identification, analysis, control, and reporting.

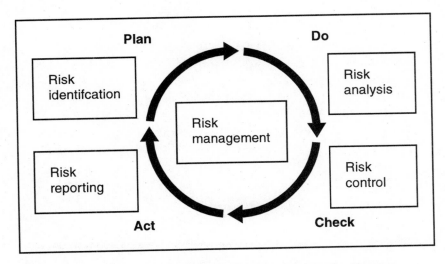

Fig 1.3 A continuous loop risk management using the Deming Wheel

Through their projects, project managers must *plan* doing risk identification, such as identifying as many risks as possible. The must *do* by performing risk analysis, such as assessing the impact of risks. They must *check* by performing risk control, such as managing the impact of risk. Finally, the must *act* by monitoring their established controls.

Risk helps mankind function more effectively and efficiently in an uncertain world. In other words, risk is a way to help respond to a series of perceptible events that could bring opportunity or havoc. Being ready for their occurrence helps us to deal confidently with their cause.

2 Project Risk: Origins and Impacts

In our book, *The People Side of Project Management*, we discussed how a project is a system consisting of various components that interact directly or indirectly (see Figure 2.1).[1]

These components consist of many items, including functions, actors, requirements, policies, procedures, goals, and objectives – interacting from a project management perspective, to accomplish one or more goals.

Project = system

The project, as a system, has an internal and external environment. The internal environment consists of components applicable to the project itself, such as actors (for example, the project manager), project procedures, project goals, and the project team. The external environment consists of components that may directly or indirectly apply to a project, such as actors (for example, senior management), company policies, and company goals. As in all systems, inputs and outputs cross the boundary between the internal and external environments. What crosses

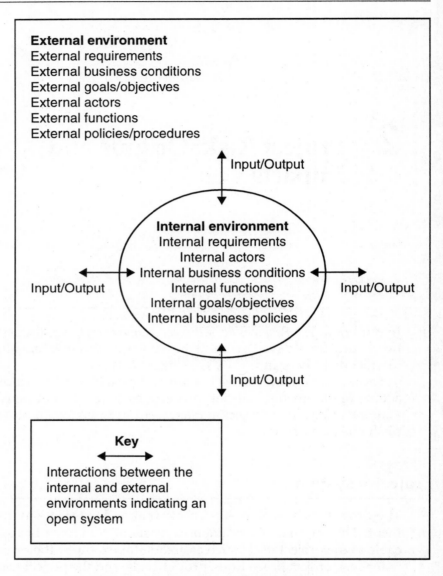

Fig 2.1   A system perspective of project management
Source: Kliem, R.L. and Ludin, I.S. (1992), *The People Side of Project Management*, Aldershot: Gower.

the boundary can be just about anything, from people to information.

When equilibrium occurs, comfort is not the only characteristic that manifests itself. Others will include:

- Assumptions become truths
- Everything is under control
- Nothing needs improvement
- Risk-taking is for fools
- Life is good

Then, something happens that causes havoc, something unanticipated occurs. The internal environment goes awry and the external environment does the same, often aggravating the former. The internal and external environments become incompatible, causing disequilibrium. When such a situation arises, managers will often be seen to be:

- Reacting rather than proacting
- Spreading blame or finger-pointing
- Replacing or demoting people
- 'Throwing' more people or money at the project
- Looking for some 'secret weapon' to save the day
- Acting like ostriches by 'sticking their heads in the sand' and hoping the situation will go away.
- Looking for new jobs

When disequilibrium arises, then the risks to projects surface. These risks can occur throughout the life cycle of a project. Disequilibriums usually create the opportunities for risks to arise because projects do not operate in an environment of *carte blanche* and unlimited resources. Several constraints are often placed on projects (see Figure 2.2).

Constraints	Disequilibriums
People: Resource poor; means more work with fewer people	Work faster, not smarter Outsourcing; morale may be poor because there are two control authorities (management and outsourced personnel)
Cost: Increased cost due to additional overtime	Reduced funding due to tight budgets Increased budget due to higher cost of outside help
Quality: Reduced quality due to fewer people responsible for proper inspections	Reduced quality due to lack of time for proper inspections Usually improved quality based on input from outsourced personnel
Schedule: Shorter schedule for product delivery	Critical milestones met without exception; work is schedule-driven, not process driven Schedule can be met due to increased resources

Fig 2.2   Constraints often placed on projects are linked to associated disequilibriums

Life cycle

The life cycle of a project consists of five simple stages: gestation, growth, independence, decline, and death (see Figure 2.3).[2]

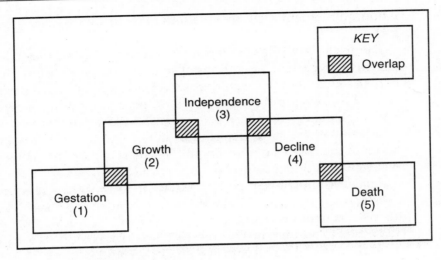

Fig 2.3   Five stages of a project
Source: Kliem, R.L. and Ludin, I.S. (1992), *The People Side of Project Management*, Aldershot: Gower.

Risks can and do arise at any given stage of a project. The earlier the stage that a risk arises, the greater will be its impact. For example, a disagreement arises over the statement of work; if the project is in the gestation stage chances are that the disagreement will threaten the project more then than it will later, such as during the independence stage.

Just as every project goes through stages, it also goes through phases (see Figure 2.4). There are five phases: feasibility, formu-

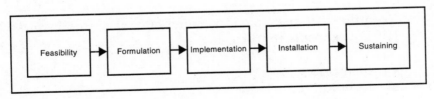

Fig 2.4   Typical phases of a project
Source: Kliem, R.L. and Ludin, I.S. (1992), *The People Side of Project Management*, Aldershot: Gower.

lation, implementation, installation, and sustaining (see Figure 2.4).[3]

The feasibility phase determines if a project is a practical alternative to current operations. The formulation phase defines in detail what the customer needs from and wants from a project as well as developing alternatives to meet those requirements. The implementation phase is the actual building of the product. The installation phase determines when the product is operational in the client's environment. The sustaining phase is when the client has direct control over the product.[4]

Risks arise at project phases – similar to those we saw with risks at project stages. However, unlike the latter, the phase when the risk occurs the greater its impact in terms of time, manpower, and effort to address it. This means that a risk is more expensive to address the later it occurs in a project schedule.

Project risk categories

From a project management perspective, risks can fall into one of four categories: cost, schedule, quality, and people (see Figure 2.5).

People risks deal with people directly or indirectly working on a project. Cost risks deal with budgeted moneys for a project. Schedule risks deal with achieving the planned schedule. Quality risks pertain to technical issues.

Exposure

Regardless of risk category, some circumstances increase the level of exposure for projects.

- Team size
- Technical complexity
- Stability of management structure
- Stability of market conditions
- Team expertise and experience

People	Cost	Schedule	Quality
Unmotivated staff; teaming	Labour overruns	Missed end deliverables	Poor workmanship
Organizational structure	Material overruns	Missed market window	Unfinished details
Responsibility for decision-making	Supply overruns	Missed critical path activities	Legal infractions
Determining how work is distributed	Monetary penalties, e.g., not meeting contractual delivery dates	Long lead times	Untested leading-edge technology

Fig 2.5 Typical project management risks by category

Team size
The larger the team size the more difficult it is to coordinate and communicate. The difficulty can increase geometrically rather than arithmetically. More people do not guarantee faster or better productivity.

Technical complexity
The more challenging the goal the greater the opportunity to fail. While challenge is important it must be feasible, especially under certain conditions at a specific point in time. For example, the sales person's promised date for technical deliverables (for example, designs, architecture, machines) does not match the 'real' delivery date of the vendor.

Stability of management structure
If management keeps changing then priorities also change. Planning under such circumstances becomes next to impossible because a baseline is impossible to achieve.

Stability of market conditions

Shooting at a moving target is difficult. The window of opportunity can move too quickly – so much so that it is impossible to achieve timely results. If the goals of a project are monumental and the market window is relatively close, then the risks are high. Project managers must take action to reduce risk.

Team expertise and experience

Members of the team must have the skills and background to perform their tasks. If a huge learning curve exists or a project is unprecedented then the stakes increase dramatically. Depending on the availability of time and the level of team expertise and experience, achieving a project success can prove quite difficult.

Typology

One way to detect the level of risk that an environment presents to a project is to use the Project Management Application Typology (PMAT). Its use will also indicate the type of environment that a project occurs in (see Figure 2.6).

The PMAT comprises four quadrants. Each one represents a specific type of environment. Two axes, or continuums, intersect to form quadrants.

The first continuum, or X-axis, reflects the degree of structure that exists in an environment. Simply stated, structure is the degree of formality that exists in an environment. Hence, more formality, more structure; less formality, less structure. An example of high structure is having many approvals to do anything. An example of low structure is the freedom to do anything; minimal approval is required, if at all.

The second continuum, or Y-axis, is the level of change that occurs in an environment. One end of the axis represents a static environment. The other end represents a dynamic, ever-changing environment.

Within each quadrant are two sub-categories to assess the level of risk that projects are posed to in a particular environ-

Dynamic Environment (DE)	**QUADRANT I (DE-LS)** **LOW PROBABILITY HIGH IMPACT**	**QUADRANT II (DE-HS)** **HIGH PROBABILITY LOW IMPACT**
Static Environment (SE)	**QUADRANT III (SE-LS)** **LOW PROBABILITY HIGH IMPACT**	**QUADRANT IV (SE-HS)** **LOW PROBABILITY LOW IMPACT**

Low Structure (LS) ◄────────► **High Structure (HS)**

Fig 2.6   Project Management Application Typology (PMAT)

ment. The first such category is whether a low or high probability of a cost, schedule, quality, or people risk can occur. The second sub-category is whether risks can have a low or high impact.

The intersection of the two axes forms four types of environment, each one reflecting a different level of risk that can affect the execution of projects. These four environments are:

- Quadrant I: Dynamic Environment – Low Structure (DE-LS)
- Quadrant II: Dynamic Environment – High Structure (DE-HS)
- Quadrant III: Static Environment – Low Structure (SE-LS)
- Quadrant IV: Static Environment – High Structure (SE-HS)

Quadrant I (Dynamic Environment – Low Structure)

This environment is typically the type where hi-tech startup companies and research and development organizations conduct their projects. Change occurs rapidly and administrative operations are often overlooked or viewed as a necessary evil. The pursuit here is the shortest path to the goal.

In this environment, the constant change presents opportunities for risk to arise. Because the implementation of project management processes will likely be at a 'working' level without much depth or formality, a high impact by cost, schedule, quality, or people risks can occur. That's because controls in place are inadequate.

Quadrant II (Dynamic Environment – High Structure)

This environment is typically the type where manufacturing firms conduct their projects. Change occurs but not as rapidly as in the Dynamic Environment – Low Structure environment. The Quadrant II environment is more stable and an appreciation for administrative operations is greater. The focus is on the means by examining multiple ways to build a product.

In this environment, the constant change environment presents opportunities for risk to arise. Because the implementation of project management processes will be at a level of depth and formality, a low impact of cost, schedule, quality, and people risks can occur.

Quadrant III (Static Environment – Low Structure)

This environment is typically the type where insurance firms conduct their projects. The environment is very stable. Both means and ends are fairly predictable and routine; administrative operations are good 'things' to do but not that important.

In this environment, stability does not present much variability to cause risk to arise. Despite the implementation of a working level of project management processes, the appearance of a risk could have a high impact. That's because any controls in place are inadequate.

Quadrant IV (Static Environment – High Structure)

This environment is typically the type where construction firms conduct their projects. The environment does not change that often; the means and the ends generally are repeatable and lend themselves to refinement in a step-by-step manner.

In this environment, stability does not present much variability to cause risks to arise. Even if risks do arise, project management processes are in place to address them.

Appropriate means

No project is an entity unto itself; it does not occur in a vacuum. A number of internal and external forces affect it, directly or indirectly. Project managers must be aware of the significant forces by looking at the potential risks that could arise and the environment that projects are conducted in. With such information, project managers can develop appropriate means to assess risks and their impacts.

3   The Psychology of Risk Management

As much psychology goes into risk management as ranking and calculating. Unfortunately, few project managers recognize this fact and, as a result, many fail to become attuned to the influence of psychology during risk management.

All in the head

Risk reflects uncertainty. Project managers, their staff, will be pursuing a path toward some goal. The path will be fraught with good and bad experiences and events. Not knowing the upcoming experiences and events, even after conducting thorough risk management, can cause considerable angst among everyone, including the person overseeing the risk management.

This psychological influence manifests itself in one of two basic ways: risk acceptance or risk aversion.

Risk acceptance
People with a risk acceptance orientation view risk as neither good nor bad but a fact of life. They therefore accept risk as it

arises and prepare for the most likely cases. Their risk management has a balanced, even optimistic, perspective. Some typical characteristics of their risk management endeavours are high-level risk assessment, cursory risk analysis, a minimal number of contingency plans, and infrequent risk monitoring.

Risk aversion

People with a risk aversion orientation view risk negatively. They dislike even the idea of risk. They often perform a thorough risk management predicated on worst-cases scenarios while simultaneously trying to address all risk situations; their risk management perspective is negative. Some typical characteristics of their risk management endeavours are a detailed risk assessment, in-depth risk analysis, elaborate contingency plans for all identified risks, and frequent risk monitoring.

These two orientations manifest themselves on individual and group levels. Each level has its unique set of factors that affect the orientation of individuals and groups towards risk and the results of any risk management exercise.

Institutional factors

Several institutional factors influence how people perceive their risk assessment. They include: atmosphere; availability of information; management style; market/economic conditions; and policies and procedures (see Figure 3.1).

Atmosphere

Every organization has a general 'atmosphere' about it. A Fortune 500 company will most likely portray a stolid, hierarchical, and highly organized approached to doing business. A small firm will most likely portray a more fluid, less hierarchical, and less organized approach to doing business. Of course, these are generalizations: some Fortune 500 companies operate like small firms while others do not fit the description, and so on. However, the point is that the atmosphere of the company influences

Factors	Risk acceptance	Risk aversion
Atmosphere	Organization is: stolid, hierarchical, highly organized	Organization is: fluid, matrix, limited structure
Availability of information	Communications in place	Communications disjointed
Management style	Receptive	Authoritarian
Market/economic conditions	Stable market	Unstable market
Policies and procedures	Relaxed environment	Restrictive environment

Fig 3.1   How people perceive risk assessment

how project managers perceive risk. If the atmosphere is stolid, hierarchical, and highly organized, risk acceptance often predominates. If the atmosphere is fluid, less hierarchical, and less organized, risk aversion often predominates.

Availability of information
Effective risk management depends on the availability of good information. If the communications infrastructure does not provide accurate and timely information, risk aversion will likely predominate. If the communications infrastructure is good, risk acceptance will likely predominate.

Management style
How management, specifically senior management, handles people will greatly affect how people view risk in general and how they approach risk management in particular. If the management style is negative, such as subscribing to a Theory X approach, risk aversion will likely predominate. If positive, such

as subscribing to a Theory Y approach, risk acceptance will likely predominate.

Market/economic conditions

If the business environment is unstable, a greater likelihood exists that risk aversion will predominate. If the business environment is stable, a greater likelihood exists that risk acceptance will predominate.

Policies and procedures

Too many policies and procedures may indicate a stifling environment. The greater their number and detail the more restrictive the work environment and greater likelihood that risk aversion will predominate. The fewer the number of policies and procedures, a greater likelihood exists that risk acceptance will predominate.

Motivation

An individual's personality influences how he or she perceives risk. Several factors influence whether a person accepts or avoids risk. Some common factors are shown in Figure 3.2.

Several studies have identified ways some or all of the factors in Figure 3.2 affect human behaviour.

- Ability
- Experience
- Knowledge
- Organizational status
- Outlook on life
- Personal goals
- Self-confidence
- Sense of commitment
- Values and beliefs

Fig 3.2   Some common factors affecting a person's attitude to risk

Abraham Maslow developed a model for understanding human motivation.[1] His model is a structure that reflects a hierarchy of needs.

- People have needs they want to satisfy.
- These needs fit into a hierarchy of importance (see Figure 3.3).
- The lower needs require satiation before higher ones.
- Any unsatisfied need creates a tension which, in turn, triggers motivation.

Frederick Herzberg's model parallels that of Maslow.[2] Herzberg developed the two factor theory of motivation: maintenance and motivational. Maintenance factors have a physical or organizational 'flavour' to them. Factors such as job security may not motivate but, if lacking, they can demotivate. Some examples of maintenance factors include company policy and administration, salary, and job security.

Needs	Definition
5. Self-actualization	Realizing one's full potential, e.g., self-motivation, morals
4. Esteem	Feeling good about one's self, e.g., confidence, independence
3. Social	Being accepted and loved, e.g., acceptance from others, acceptance of others
2. Safety	Being protected from harm, e.g., freedom from persecution, law and order
1. Physiological	Satisfying basic biological needs, e.g., hunger, thirst

Fig 3.3 Maslow's hierarchy of needs

Motivational factors have a psychological flavour to them. They encourage high levels of motivation when present. Some examples of motivational factors include achievement, recognition, and advancement.

A person's sense of achievement can also influence their perception of risk and how they approach risk management. David McClelland developed the *n*-Ach, or *need for achievement factor*, for motivation.[3] He noted that some people have a greater desire or need for achievement than do others. Depending on the degree of this need, people will endure hardships and other obstacles if their need to achieve is strong and their belief that success will bring the appropriate reward: for example, working long hours on a medical research project to find a cure for cancer.

Cassidy and Lynn illustrate that risk implies a need for achievement, that risks are challenges to be met and dealt with.[4] People have wants that need fulfilment; risks are catalysts that motivate people to achieve. Elements that comprise those wants are shown in Figure 3.4.[5]

Victor Vroom has demonstrated how the goals of individuals influence their behaviour along with the probability that their

```
● Acquisition – obtaining enormous wealth

● Competition – competing and coming out in first place

● Master – achieving high standards

● Excellence – doing the best with what you have

● Status – getting to the top and controlling others

● Work ethic – knowing performance is its own merit
```

Fig 3.4   Risk implies a need for achievement
Source: Cassidy, T and Lynn, R (1989), *Journal of Occupational Psychology*, Vol. 62, pp.301–12.

behaviour will lead to goal achievement.[6] The key is the perception that a certain behaviour will attain a goal. Hence, if an individual believes that his or her behaviour will bring the reward of achieving personal goals then he or she will act in a specific manner. If that person does not perceive that a certain behaviour will achieve goals then he or she will be less inclined to behave in a certain way. So, if the goals of the individual and the goals of the organization are the same then the individual will exhibit the desired behaviour.

B. F. Skinner's model of human behaviour helps to determine the perception of risk and the results of risk management.[7] Skinner addressed the issue of modification on the effects of the environment regarding human behaviour. His model views human behaviour as a stimulus–response relationship and illustrates that, through conditioning, a desired behaviour will result. Such behaviour occurs either positively or negatively. Positive reinforcement occurs when the frequency of response increases due to something positive (such as a monetary reward) being provided. Negative reinforcement occurs when the frequency of a response occurs due to the removal of a negative event (such as pain).

The above theories of human motivation are instrumental in our understanding of how project managers perceive risk. It is quite likely that project managers will perceive risk positively if the environment rewards risk taking. They will view risk more positively if rewards exist, if the possibility of receiving them is high, or if the consequences of failure are minimal. Project managers will view risk even more positively if management encourages risk taking. Risk will be viewed negatively if management discourage risk taking. See Figure 3.5 for a summary of the theories discussed.

When individuals become members of groups, a number of factors can influence their perception of risk and, in turn, can affect the group's own perception of risk. These factors are shown in Figure 3.6.

Several studies have identified ways these and other factors affect the behaviour of people in groups and of the groups themselves.

Maslow	5. Self-actualization 4. Esteem 3. Social 2. Safety 1. Physiological
McClelland	Achievement (*n*-Ach)
Cassidy and Lynn	● Acquisition ● Competition ● Master ● Excellence ● Status ● Work ethic
Vroom	Goals influence behaviour
Skinner	Issue modification

Fig 3.5   Theories and theorists of human motivation

● Cohesiveness
● Confidence in others
● Group goals
● Mores
● Norms
● Pecking order
● Rituals
● Self-reference

Fig 3.6   Factors influencing perception of risk

The 'groupthink' theory of Irving Janis is a way of thinking that occurs within highly cohesive groups.[8] Groups experiencing groupthink put considerable pressure on individuals until unanimity occurs which, in turn, affects judgement by individuals and the group. This pressure for consensus results in filtering information and limiting courses of action to consider and to pursue. In the end, groupthink restricts decision-making.

Using college students, Solomon Asch conducted experiments showing how group pressure affects opinions and attitudes[9] and revealed that group pressure can have a substantial influence on group decision-making and the acknowledgement of different ideas. Asch noticed that when a group member was confronted with only one person of an opposite opinion then he would not change his response. However, when the person hav-

Denial	Appearing not to recognize a threat
Displacement	Not reacting predictably to a given situation, but reacting instead based on another situation
Projection	Rather than accept responsibility for a given situation, laying blame on others
Reaction	Behaviour opposite of previous patterns
Regression	Moving back into an old pattern of behaviour when dealing with events today that are similar in nature
Repression	Consciously removing an event from memory
Suppression	Unconsciously removing an event from memory

Fig 3.7   Personality factors which negatively bias individuals when calculating risk

ing the opposite opinion was supported by another person the group member yielded to their pressure by changing his opinion.

The point here is that social forces exert considerable pressure on individuals to conform to values and beliefs. This pressure can result in individuals holding either a positive or negative perception of risk, depending on that held by the group of which they are a member. The desire for consensus and conformity can therefore strongly influence judgements by project managers dealing with risk. If the project team has a negative perception of risk, chances are that the project manager will feel pressure to feel likewise; otherwise, a clash will surely arise during project execution. See Figure 3.7 for personality factors which negatively bias people.

Balancing act

Whether on an individual or group level, therefore, project managers must maintain a balanced view of risk and maintain that balance throughout risk management. There are many ways to achieve this, including:

- Brainstorming
- Delphi approach
- Mind Mapping®
- Outside opinion
- Scientific method

Brainstorming

Project managers can use this simple technique to help them maintain an objective perception of risk. The project manager assembles a group of experts. Without any screening, the group generate ideas about a topic and list them. While generating the list, no criticism of any idea is allowed. Content to have identified everything, the group removes 'insignificant' or 'irrelevant' ideas from the list until satisfied. This approach is excellent for generating lists of threats, processes, and controls when conducting risk identification and analysis.

Delphi approach

This technique is used to obtain an independent opinion on a topic of choice by consulting with subject-matter experts. The project manager designs a questionnaire and submits it to experts for their opinion. The results are tabulated and returned to the experts for revision of their opinion. Experts with extreme opinions (that is, ones outside the norm) are asked to explain their position. This approach is excellent for offsetting groupthink and allows for greater independent thinking during risk identification and analysis.

Mind Mapping®

A non-linear approach to identify the linkage between thoughts, or concepts, Mind Mapping® allows the mind to identify its associative concepts using graphics. This technique is excellent when used by individuals or groups to identify the major and minor concepts supporting an idea. The project manager can use Mind Mapping® to identify risks and their relationship to one another during risk assessment.

Outside opinion

The 'outsider' could be a consultant either outside or within the organization. The idea is to obtain an 'outsider's' viewpoint. This approach is excellent if the consultant has a solid reputation for objectivity and expertise and is able to identify issues that individuals or a group within an organization would never see. The consultant will see the 'big picture' and is not emotionally attached to the project.

Scientific method

This technique forces objectivity in performing risk management. It involves these simple steps:

- Defining the problem
- Analysing the problem
- Collecting data
- Analysing data
- Developing solutions

- Testing solutions
- Obtaining feedback

Scientific method has existed for centuries and, despite its variations, provides an effective way to ensure discipline in an individual's approach. It is excellent in achieving results where objectives, processes, and threats of risk identification and analysis are vague or ill-defined.

Psychology + maths = risk management

Managing risk is as much psychology as it is mathematics. Whether on an individual or group level, perception and approach to risk influence the results of a risk management exercise. Project managers who recognize this will inevitably achieve better risk management and project performance targets.

4 Decision-making and Risk Management

Good risk management requires good decision-making. Both require focusing on how to best achieve the goals of a project under conditions of uncertainty. Both require making trade-offs based upon what is most to least important. Both require considering some element of probability in achieving goals and the occurrence of some events and, based upon that information, determining the appropriate actions to take. Risk management and decision-making are like tea and crumpets: in the right amount they go well together.

Right decisions

Good decision-making – that is, accomplishing the right goals efficiently and effectively – incorporates several characteristics.

- It is timely. Project managers must make a decision at the right time. Failure to make a timely decision only increases the risk and the impact to a project. Schedules slide. Moneys become unavailable. Quality declines. Morale plummets.

- It is objective. An objective decision relies on facts and data, not the prejudicial whim of project managers. This does not discount the importance of 'gut feeling', or intuitive decision; even these are based on some facts and data, albeit incomplete.
- It is rational. A logic exists behind a decision; some type of rationale exists. Even with an intuitive decision, there is the rationale of a decision based upon some driving force.
- It is purposeful. Project managers make a decision to achieve a goal or an objective. Their projects must accomplish something, either from a short- or long-term perspective.

Ingredients

Unfortunately, not all decisions are the right ones. Whether a decision is good or poor (not accomplishing its intent is one) is determined by several factors:

- Analysis paralysis
- Behavioural sway
- Bias
- Incomplete facts and data
- Institutional constraints
- Misinterpretation
- Overly aggressive or conservative reactions
- Wrong analogy

Analysis paralysis
In most cases, project managers have plenty of facts and data to review before making a decision. Sometimes, manipulating facts and data takes so long and is so convoluted that they find the only sensible thing to do is to perform more analysis. Analysis paralysis sets in and all hope for making a decision fades as procrastination takes over.

Behavioural sway

Project managers can make poor decisions due to pressures from senior individuals or from peers. This indicates a lack of confidence, for whatever reason, to exercise independent judgement. In other words, they 'cave in' to pressure.

Bias

Many people make decisions based upon beliefs, values, or paradigms that can place 'blinders' on them. They use a value screen that filters in data that only supports their way of thinking or doing business. In the end, they hear only what they want, not need, to hear.

Incomplete facts and data

Many instances occur where a project manager must make decisions based on minimal data. A lack of facts and data can result in erroneous, inefficient, or ineffective decisions. Decision-making under such circumstances may be due to laziness or the inability to acquire additional requisite facts and data. Either way, the consequences can lead to serious problems during a project.

Institutional constraints

Project managers face many constraints, often more than functional managers. They frequently lack 'command and control' over team members, their budgets are dependent on senior management's generosity, and marketing forces can dramatically impact on their project's fate. Depending on the extent of the constraints, project managers can find themselves pushed or rushed into making poor decisions.

Misinterpretation

The more complex the project, the easier it is to misinterpret facts and data. Many project managers in a rush to trim expenditures or meet a milestone in a schedule may interpret facts and data incorrectly. That misinterpretation, ironically, can aggravate circumstances. For example, project managers may attribute poor performance to a morale problem when the actual cause is lack of training.

Overly aggressive or conservative reactions

Project managers make poor decisions because they jump to conclusions, or they wait too long and make an overly cautious decision. Either way, their decision can be a poor one due to timing.

Wrong analogy

Analogies are great tools for teaching but, if used incorrectly, they can mislead. Similarly, if project managers pick the wrong analogy to assess a situation they, too, can make the wrong decision.

Two types of decision

Decision-making is a complex process. However, it is possible to differentiate between two types of decisions that project managers can make: routine and non-routine.

Routine decisions appear often, have predictable results, and are handled according to a standard operating procedure. They require minimum effort and thinking to develop a solution. Risks are traditionally low and not much time is spent on determining the outcome or course of events for 'what if' scenarios. A typical routine decision is a project manager responding to a request for information regarding a task in the schedule.

Non-routine decisions do not appear often, lack precedents for their handling, and the results are derived only through an educated guess. Their handling requires taking a general problem-solving approach as well as creativity. Risks here are traditionally medium or high depending on the complexity of the activity. A typical non-routine decision is devising a way to improve the schedule performance of a task on the critical path. Figure 4.1 depicts risk versus decision type. The more routine the decision, the lower the risk for making a poor choice; the more non-routine the decision, the higher the risk.

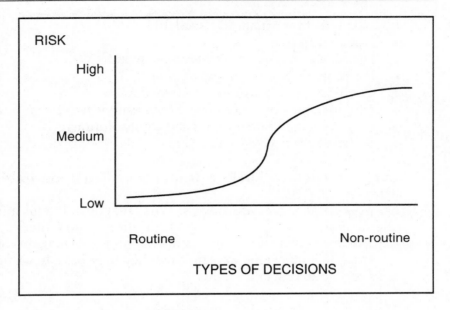

Fig 4.1 Risk versus decision type

Roundabout

In the project environment, the Deming Wheel (see Chapter 1) can help project managers to handle these two types of decision. As we saw earlier, using the Deming Wheel consists of four processes for decision-making: plan, do, check, act.

Plan is determining the goals, objectives, requirements, and plans of a project. *Do* is executing the results of the first process. *Check* is tracking and monitoring performance to determine adherence to the plan. *Act* is taking the necessary corrective actions to adhere to the plan. The Deming Wheel is a circle that continues throughout the life of a project.

Using the Deming Wheel, decision-makers should remember the following keys for effective decision-making when performing risk management:

- Every decision will have a desirable and undesirable effect

- No perfect information is available
- Not all information is equal
- Decisions are a means rather than an end
- Decision criteria are essential
- Conditional values or events are valuable
- The presumption of a causal relationship is necessary
- Computer software tools are aids, not solutions
- A strategy is necessary to achieve goals

Every decision will have a desirable and an undesirable effect

No project managers are islands. What they decide will affect one or more processes and results. In other words, there's no free lunch on any project. For example, if project managers want to complete a milestone date on time they may have to assume risks related to cost and quality.

No perfect information is available

Ideally, project managers should have enough information to make the right decisions. Unfortunately, that circumstance rarely arises. At a minimum, however, they need to answer these seven questions before making an important decision, especially a non-routine one:

- Who?
- What?
- When?
- Where?
- Why?
- How?
- How much?

As there is a tradeoff between the level of uncertainty regarding a decision and the time and cost expended to gather the right amount of information, the more non-routine and uncertainty surrounding a decision the more time and money project managers should spend on gathering information. The more routine the decision, the less time and money they need to spend.

Not all information is equal
Information is valuable in degrees. Information that reduces the uncertainty surrounding a non-routine decision is more important than information that confirms a fact already known. What are the important issues and what information will address them efficiently and effectively is the requirement here. For example, risks affecting tasks on the critical path is more important than ones not on it.

Decisions are a means rather than an end
Decisions are not important by themselves. They are made to accomplish something or satisfy a need; otherwise, a decision is really unnecessary. Making a decision is not, however, enough by itself. It requires follow-through. That is, project managers must ensure execution of the decision. For example, the project manager replans a new schedule; he or she must then ensure that the project team follows the new schedule and not the old one.

Decision criteria are essential
The best way to minimize bias or subjectivity in decision-making is to develop a criterion to make the appropriate decision. Being a human invention, the criterion will never be totally free of bias. It will, however, be a more rational basis for making a decision. For example, it can consist of a mathematical formula or a set of assumptions for ranking risks that affect critical areas.

Conditional values or events are valuable
When project managers make a decision they often have several scenarios to consider. Each scenario will have a certain result based upon achieving a certain value or a certain event happening. By knowing the outcomes of several scenarios project managers can decide the most appropriate way to respond. For example, a project manager might identify different schedule risks and develop contingency plans to respond to them.

The presumption of a causal relationship is necessary
When making a decision, it is best to assume that the final results must have a direct relationship with the decision.

Otherwise, the decision occurs in a void and serves no purpose. The idea is to make a decision that will have a specific effect, either partially or completely. The investment of time, effort, and expense in a decision minus the resulting gain is called a payoff, or the utility of an outcome. For example, the project manager invests considerable time and effort in hiring an outside consultant to conduct risk analysis rather than having the work done internally.

Computer software tools are aids, not solutions
Computer software tools are produced and used at a rapid pace. Schedulers, estimators, and risk management packages can all be obtained as software. Although results are provided based on inputs to these packages, a need exists to understand the real meaning of what is generated. People make decisions; software only aids the decision-maker to determine what options look best.

A strategy is necessary to achieve goals
Strategy involves determining the best approach to achieve goals, selecting the most appropriate tools or techniques, such as cost analysis, linear programming, simulation, or statistical analysis. For example, project managers select the right tool or technique, such as PERT estimating technique or Monte Carlo simulation, for risk analysis. The tool or technique provides the means to determine what disciplines are necessary to achieve the specific goals of a project.

A good strategy is, however, more than the employment of a tool or technique. Several other considerations apply. Some of these are discussed in this section. Strategy requires a model, or construct, of how the environment works or should work. For example, a descriptive model describes how the environment operates in an 'as is' perspective, concentrating on the decision-maker's knowledge, experience, assumptions, and beliefs. An alternative is a normative, or prescriptive, model describing how the environment should operate, a 'to be' perspective. This, too, is based on the decision-maker's knowledge, experience, assumptions, and beliefs.

Both models can be highly mathematical and objective or very intuitive and subjective. Project managers can perform a risk analysis based on a descriptive or prescriptive model.

In all good strategies there is the requirement to identify and select alternatives that yield a value for some predetermined goal. Will it achieve 100 per cent of a goal or 50 per cent? Will it save or generate US $50,000 or US $100,000? The significant concern here is to identify the different alternatives and determine the payoff for each. Which alternative gives the most payoff? The least? None? For example, project managers can develop a series of contingency plans which mitigate weaknesses to different degrees for a risk identified during risk analysis.

The preparation of a strategy should include a method to monitor its effectiveness. Project managers should review any deviations from its intent and what is actually occurring, so as to identify the cause and take appropriate action. For example, they will ensure that certain processes have been implemented after conducting a risk analysis.

Finally, any strategy requires a formal, methodical approach to decision-making. However, project managers should not discount the impact of intuition. Facts and data may indicate that the strategy is working yet a 'gut feel' may indicate quite the contrary. Many top executives have made decisions based upon intuition and succeeded. Project managers may find that the facts and data acquired during risk analysis indicate a low probability of occurrence. Yet, their intuition suggests that the risk could have a high probability of occurrence and have a big impact on the project. Conventional wisdom dictates that some risk control measures should exist.

Bi-level

Decision-making occurs on one of two levels: individual and group. Each level has pluses and minuses.

At an individual level, decision-making tends to be quick and efficient, unless the decision-maker is indecisive. Deliberation within groups requires 'give and take' which requires both time and the repetition of thoughts to attain consensus.

However, not everything is positive when decision-making is on the individual level. Individual decision-makers can easily incorporate bias into their decisions, claiming objectivity when actually being highly subjective. Individuals can also have a narrow focus, thereby being unable to see the 'big picture'. They can also find it difficult to implement their decision because people lack any ownership of it.

Decision-making by groups has its advantages in comparison with decisions made at individual level. Groups tend to incorporate less bias in their decisions, unless they suffer from groupthink. They often look at the big picture because individuals challenge one another. Studies show that groups tend to take higher risks than individuals. For example, a group of executives deciding whether a specific technology should be in place to support their proposed product. As a group they may decide to accept the high risks. As individual decision-makers they may be less inclined to do so. This is attributed to a spread of responsibility over a group as opposed to a single point of contact, in other words, one person. Each group player feels less responsible for any potential loss, because responsibility is spread over the group. The group also finds it easier to implement their decision because more people have ownership in its creation and adoption.

Group decision-making is not totally positive as groups require a period of deliberation in order to come to a consensus and that lengthens the time taken to come to a decision. This can place pressure on members to reach agreement, thereby stifling disagreement.

Finally, groups are inefficient because not only do they take extra time but also require more resources, for example, room size and supplies. See Figure 4.2 for risk tendencies and reduction when groups make decisions.

High risk tendency	Reducing high risk tendency
Overly optimistic due to 'group' illusion of invulnerability	Conclusions are based on facts and data
'Group' wisdom overtakes moral and ethical conduct	Sanity check for decisions is tested against external unbiased sources
Insulation from outside sources	Individuals' differing expressions are not discounted or considered disloyal to the group
Introduction of new information may be disregarded because group has made up its mind	Group rules of order include opportunities to disagree or criticize ideas and plans
Individual dissension is limited based on 'wholeness and size' of the group (high probability of ostracizing the dissenter)	Criticism is tolerated by both group leaders and members Group leaders' expectations are not voiced at the beginning of the meeting

Fig 4.2 Risk tendencies and reduction when groups make decisions

Back to reality

Remember that a decision has only two kinds of outcome – those that are expensive to fix and those that are not.

Risk management is good decision-making. Planning, doing, checking, and acting are common activities during risk identification, analysis, control, and reporting. Poor decision-making, therefore, is poor risk management. That, in turn, means poor quality, slipped milestones, overrun budgets, and low morale. In other words, poor project performance.

Part II
The Risk Management Process

5 Step One: Risk Identification

As we have already seen, there are four steps to risk management. Risk identification is the first of them.

Purpose

Risk identification entails researching the project to determine its components and risks. The purpose of this exercise is:

- To identify the most significant participants in risk management and to provide the basis for subsequent management.
- To stabilize the groundwork by providing all the necessary information to conduct risk analysis efficiently and effectively. Poor results from risk identification often mean the equivalent outcomes from risk analysis.
- To identify the pieces of the system or project being studied. For example, a component might be a process (such as developing a schedule).
- To identify the inherent risks in a project. An example of risk might be not developing meaningful schedules.

Identifying the most significant participants

Project managers must look not only at the information for doing risk identification but also at the personnel carrying out the project, throughout the organization. This is vital when setting the groundwork. They should specifically identify people, not only 'core team' members but also senior managers and clients. Eventually, they must identify anyone who provides crucial information for performing risk identification and analysis steps.

Project managers should select people who have a good knowledge of the business and technical aspects of the project as well as the goals and risk confronting it. They must recognize that these people should also have good communications and team-building skills – skills which are essential for sharing information and identifying risk. Risk identification is, more often than not, the product of a good collaborative effort among several individuals, rather than one project manager.

Stabilizing groundwork

Considerable groundwork goes into conducting the risk identification even though it involves answering a simple question: 'What information is necessary to conduct the identification?'

Understanding the components, goals, and risks confronting a project is not trivial. Such an understanding affects the extent or depth that risk analysis will eventually take. The more information, not data, available the better the risk analysis produced. Information is transformed data, of course, meaning that the information is relevant, accurate, and reliable in the format the requester needs.

Information may or may not be readily available. Figure 5.1 lists some items to review for information. The way to find the right information is to know what is wanted; what is available; where to obtain it; who to get if from; and when to receive it. To collate all this information requires a good understanding of policies and procedures, the organizational structure, and information architecture of the company.

- Cost and time estimates
- Data bases (manual and automatic)
- Disaster recovery plans
- Implementation plans
- Memorandums
- Organization charts
- Policy statements
- Product literature
- Project manuals
- Project plans
- Resources histograms
- Schedules
- Statement of work
- Statistics and metrics
- Technical documentation

Fig 5.1   Sources of information

Identifying the pieces

After collecting the information, project managers identify the components or processes of the project and its risks or goals.

When identifying components, project managers frequently try to 'explode' everything into individual pieces. Such an attempt results in frustrating everyone participating in the risk identification step. The best method is to view each component as not being mutually exclusive but having overlapping relationships. And the best way to visualize this concept is by using Venn diagrams (see Figure 5.2).[1] With physical items – and other discrete items, such as a computing system – project managers can treat the components as mutually exclusive. With processes and other non-discrete concepts then the division between components is not so distinct because they overlap. The overlap is fine as long as everyone doing risk identification recognizes its existence.

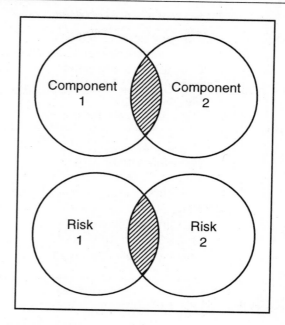

Fig 5.2   Venn diagrams showing conceptual overlap of components and risks

Identifying inherent risks

Identifying goals and risks of projects follow the same pattern as processes. Project managers must recognize that not all goals and risks are equal regardless of perspective. Their relationships overlap, as illustrated in Figure 5.2 Goals are more discrete than risks and, not surprisingly, prioritizing them is easier. However, identifying risks can pose a problem because one risk can be closely related to another and, therefore, overlap.

When identifying risks, project managers will be helped by a list of common risks facing almost any project. Figure 5.3 lists some common risks that threaten most projects.

Project managers can take one of two approaches towards identifying components. They can do it themselves or with a group.

Phases of project management	Common risks
Leading	• High turnover of critical team members • Indecisiveness • Lack of client 'buy-in'/involvement • Lack of senior management support • Lack of team consensus over project plans • Limited authority/control for project manager • No project vision • No team-building • Poor communications • Poor motivation of participants
Definition	• High technological complexity • Ill-defined goals and objectives • Ill-defined project scope • Changing requirements • Incomplete or ill-defined requirements • Incomplete statement of work • Unrealistic goals
Planning	• Inaccurate cost estimates • Inaccurate time estimates • Incomplete project plan • Incomplete work breakdown structure • No formal estimating tools • No historical precedence for project • Poor allocation of resources • Unrealistic schedules
Organizing	• Inadequate communications infrastructure in place • Lack of resources • Lack of subject matter expertise • No documented procedures/processes • Poor assignment/allocation of tasks • Too complex for resources available • Wrong selection of project management software
Controlling	• Little or no project management process in place • No impact analysis of changes • Inflexibility of project plans • Constantly changing market conditions • Poor assessment of project results • Unsatisfactory conduct of status review meetings • Lack of change management • Inability to take timely corrective action
Closure	• Unable to capture results • Incomplete winding down of activities

Fig 5.3   Common project risks

If they identify components by themselves, the phase can go quite quickly. However, this approach is prone to several shortcomings, including taking a narrow perspective and injecting false assumptions. Ways to overcome this are:

- Cross-checking the results with subject matter experts
- Comparing results with that of other projects of a similar nature
- Applying techniques like brainstorming (see Chapter 3)

- People
    - Facilitator
    - Scribe
    - Subject matter experts
    - Team members

- Equipment
    - Easel pad stand
    - Overhead projector/spare bulbs
    - Pointing device
    - Whiteboard

- Supplies
    - Easel pads
    - Erasers
    - Pens/markers
    - Viewfoils

- Facilities
    - Layout of table and chairs
    - Lighting
    - Size of room
    - Temperature

Fig 5.4 List of considerations for conducting risk assessment sessions

Error	Description
Accidental	Didn't want it to happen
Additions	Add something that shouldn't be
Deletions	Remove something that shouldn't be
Detections	Unable to recognize
Emotional	Being caught up in feelings
Inspections	Visual inaccuracies
Interpretations	Misunderstood meanings
Mental	Being fatigued
Omissions	Overlook something that is needed
Ordering	Choose incorrect order of actions
Perception	How others perceive you
Perspective	Knowing yourself
Physical	Poor placement, spacing, size
Purposeful	Deliberate violations
Quality	Meeting with predetermined expectations
Recall	Being forgetful
Reversals	Choosing wrong direction
Selections	Make incorrect choice
Spiritual	Inappropriate behaviour based on a higher plane
Substitutions	Incorrect replacement
Timing	Being too early or too late
Transcendental	Unintentionally carrying over habits from one sequence of behaviour to another
Unintentional	Didn't mean to happen

Fig 5.5 Taxonomy of human errors

If they identify components as a group, project managers have a better opportunity to create a more balanced, complete identification. If managed correctly, groups will challenge assumptions and ideas. If not, several shortcomings are likely to occur, including suppressing unpopular ideas and providing narrow coverage. Ways to overcome this are:

- Comparing results with that of other projects of a similar nature
- Applying good facilitation and effective listening skills (see Figure 5.4)
- Applying techniques such as scientific method (see Chapter 3)

Whichever approach is taken, whether individual or group, remember that human error remains a factor. Human beings are prone to oversights on occasion. Just being aware of human error enables better decision-making, as outside influences remain accounted for. See Figure 5.5 for a list and brief description of types of human errors.

Prioritizing the pieces

When determining priority, project managers must recognize that not everything is equal, regardless of perspective taken (for example, financial, legal, functionality). A good systems perspective can help project managers understand how all pieces fit together and further help them determine which piece is more important *vis-à-vis* another. 'Structural functional' is the term for describing this perspective because it recognizes that each component plays a role – albeit some more important than others. For example, a schedule is typically more important than having project procedures.

Project managers can take several approaches towards prioritizing components, risks, and goals. They can do it by themselves or with a group. The same considerations are applicable to prioritizing as with identifying them.

When prioritizing components, risks, and goals, project managers must keep in mind that as a project progresses down a life cycle the importance of a risk declines and other risks gain ascendancy (see Figure 5.6). For example, risk 1 (solid line) is relevant until risk 2 comes into play, and so on. The dotted lines in Figure 5.6 indicate the end of a risk (e.g., risk 1) at the entrance of a new one, e.g., risk 2. The reason is that the circumstances change over time, making some risks no longer relevant. Thus, if a project has progressed into the production phase, poor definition of requirements has less importance than ensuring that the pieces are functional. This situation necessitates continual risk monitoring throughout the life cycle of a project.

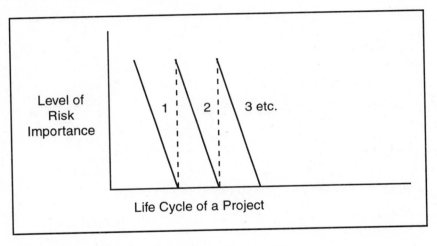

Fig 5.6   Level of importance of a risk over time

Building confidence

Project managers should take risk identification very seriously. Not only does it set the stage for better decision-making during the later steps of risk management but also it builds confidence among team members. Recognition of this enables the project manager to identify all the significant risks to the project, thereby setting the stage for successful project execution.

6 Step Two: Risk Analysis

The second step of risk management is risk analysis. To describe it, we have divided this chapter into four sections: Section 1 is the introduction; Section 2 provides an overview of statistics; Section 3 describes some risk analysis techniques; and the last section is the conclusion.

Section 1 Introduction

Several techniques are available to conduct risk analysis. Some are easier to apply than others. In this chapter we provide an explanation of these techniques.

Section 2 Statistics

Statistics play an important role in risk analysis. The purpose of this section is to familiarize the reader with general statistics principles and techniques to better understand risk analysis techniques.

The example used is the ABC Company, which is an oil supply house, consisting of ten employees. Let us use two variables: oil demand for the winter season and the number of weeks in the winter season for a growing rural community. These two variables explain the basic topics of statistics:

- Frequency distributions
- Mean, median, and mode
- Standard deviation
- Normal distribution
- Probability

Raw data is collected for the number of barrels of oil used and the number of weeks of winter in the community and entered into a database. The database currently has 100 sets of data for each variable.

Frequency distributions

Collections of large amounts of raw data are usually summarized in a frequency distribution. A tabular chart (see Figure 6.1) is one way to identify this distribution and to determine the variables. Place them into 'classes,' and calculate the number of times each class occurs based on raw data. This tabular chart is called a frequency distribution, or frequency table.

A histogram graphically depicts the frequency distribution that consists of sets of rectangles, as shown in Figure 6.2. A line chart is simply a plot of the histogram using a line to connect the data points as opposed to using sets of rectangles, as shown in Figure 6.3

Mean, median, and mode

The 'average' is a word used often. 'What's the average temperature? What's the average rainfall? What's the average stock value for XYZ company?' and so on. Most people don't realize that 'average' can have more than one definition; what they mean is 'the value that typically represents a set of data'. However, three averages exist from a statistical standpoint: the mean, median, and mode.

Barrels of oil used/week	Number of times used
250	0
275	2
300	20
325	15
350	9
375	4
400	24
425	6
450	1
475	5
500	11
525	3
	Total = 100

Fig 6.1   Frequency table

The mean is the sum of an array of numbers divided by the number of instances. For example, the set of numbers, 2 , 4, 6, 8, 10 has a mean of 6, calculated by adding the set (2 + 4 + 6 + 8 + 10 = 30) and dividing it by 5 (the number of instances) which equals 6. Mathematically, the representation is: The average = $S(X)/N$, where N is a set of numbers from X_1 through X_N and S is read as 'the sum of'.

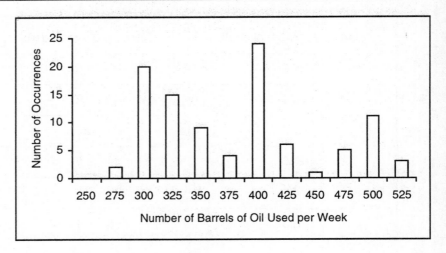

Fig 6.2   Histogram

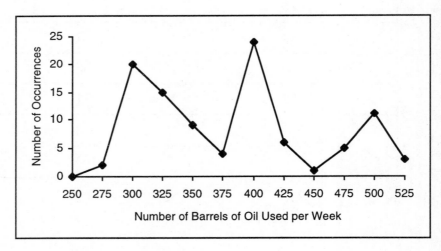

Fig 6.3   Line drawing

When using weight factors a 'weighted mean' can be calculated: for example, in conducting a survey of customer satisfaction for the ABC Company. One hundred people were queried to choose a rating from excellent to poor, with 5 being excellent and 1 poor. The following table shows the distribution:

(a) Customer satisfaction	(b) Rating	(c) Number of people	(d) (b) × (c)
Excellent	5	60	300
Average	3	35	105
Poor	1	5	5
		Total 100	410

Calculations start by multiplying the 'Rating' by the 'Number of people' who agree. For example, the excellent rating of 5 has 60 people who agree. Thus, 5 times 60 equals 300 (column d above). Completed calculations for the other ratings are shown and then added together. The total is 410 which is divided by the 100 participants giving a value of 4.1. This weighted mean is midway between an average (3) and an excellent (5) rating. Mathematically, the representation is: the weighted mean = $S(WX_N)/S(W)$ where N is a set of numbers from X_1 through X_N, w is the weighting factor of numbers from X_1 through X_N and S is read as 'sum of'.

The median (or average) is defined as the middle number of a set of numbers when arranged according to magnitude. For example, take the set of nine numbers: 2, 2, 3, 3, 4, 5, 5, 6, and 10. The median, or middle number, is 4. For another example, take the set of six numbers 3, 4, 5, 6, 7, and 8 yields a median of 5.5 [(5 + 6)/2].

The mode is the number that occurs most frequently within a set of numbers. For example, take the set of numbers 2, 2, 3, 4, 5, 5, 5, 6, and 7. It has a mode of 5 (because it occurs most). For another example take the set 2, 3, 7, 9, 11, 15. It has no mode at all. The last example is the set 3, 3, 5, 8, 9, 11, 11, 15, and 20. This set has two modes, 3 and 11.

Using the mean, median, and mode to determine the 'average' depends on what to achieve. For example, how many times is a book checked out of a library? Use the mode as the average. Which brand of automobile is preferred by consumers? Consider using the mean.

Be careful when deciding which 'average' to use to indicate results. The following example illustrates the caveat. ABC Company is making an annual salary survey. It is a small company, having only ten employees, including its president. The salaries per year are:

- President (1 person)   US$100 K
- Vice-presidents (2)   US$ 85 K
- Managers (2)   US$ 75 K
- Staff (3)   US$ 35 K
- Administrative (2)   US$ 20 K

The task is to determine the average salary for ABC Company due to rumours that the entire staff, except the president, is about to leave because of low salaries. The president can use the mean, median, or mode to determine the average salary. Using the mean yields an average salary of US$63 K (100 + 85 + 75 + 35 + 20 divided by 5). A weighted mean, however, might provide a better result. Using a weighted mean, the average salary is US$56.5 [(1 × 100) + (2 × 85) + (2 × 75) + (3 × 35) + (2 × 20) divided by 10]. The median is US$55 K[1/2 × (75 + 35)]. The mode is US$35 K.

Summarized, the average salary could be chosen as:

- US$63.0 K   using the mean
- US$56.5 K   using the weighted mean
- US$55.0 K   using the median
- US$35.0 K   using the mode

Standard deviation

The spread of data about an average value is called variation. Several ways exist to measure this variation. Range is one way. It is simply taking the difference between the largest and smallest numbers in the dataset. The range for the numbers 3, 4, 5, 7, 11, 11, 12, 15, 15, and 17 is 14 (17 minus 3). Some people choose to call the range as the lowest to the highest number and in this case it is 3–17.

Standard deviation is another value that measures dispersion about the mean. The standard deviation equals the square root of the sum of each data point minus the mean squared and divided by the number of data points. Mathematically the expression is shown as:

$$s = \sqrt{S\ (X_i - \text{Mean})^2/N}$$

where s is the standard deviation, X_i is each data point, and N is the number of data points. Note: When frequencies or weights are attached to the X_is, the mathematical expression above becomes:

$$s = \sqrt{S\ f_i\ (X_i - \text{Mean})^2/N}$$ where f_i are frequencies or weights.

Solving for the standard deviation in the example above yields:

N = 10 (data points)
Mean = 3 + 4 + 5 + 7 + 11 + 11 + 12 + 15 + 15 + 17 = 100/10 = 10

$S(X_i - \text{Mean})^2/N$ is:

$$
\begin{array}{lcr}
(3-10)^2/10 & = & 4.90 \\
(4-10)^2/10 & = & 3.60 \\
(5-10)^2/10 & = & 2.50 \\
(7-10)^2/10 & = & .90 \\
(11-10)^2/10 & = & .10 \\
(11-10)^2/10 & = & .10 \\
(12-10)^2/10 & = & .40 \\
(15-10)^2/10 & = & 2.50 \\
(15-10)^2/10 & = & 2.50 \\
(17-10)^2/10 & = & \underline{4.90} \\
\text{Total} & & 22.40
\end{array}
$$

The square root of 22.40 = 4.73

For a normal distribution this means that 68.27 per cent of all data points are included within one standard deviation (plus or minus one standard deviation from the mean).

Another way to understand the standard deviation is when shopping to purchase a package of meat with a label that reads 1.0 kilograms. In reality the package does not exactly weigh one kilogram, only approximately. The question is 'How close?' It might really weigh 1.2 kilograms or even 0.75 kilograms. If weighing more, the consumer is happy, because he gets more than he paid for. If it weighs less, the consumer is unhappy, because he paid for more than he received. The supplier has similar pluses and minuses. The standard deviation helps to focus on the dispersion about the average. The smaller the standard deviation, the better chance that the meat weighs one kilogram.

Normal distribution

The normal distribution is the traditional bell-shaped curve of a graph (see Figure 6.4). It has a mean of 0 and a standard deviation of 1. Educators have relied for years on this distribution to assign grades. How to determine who gets an A or an F is usually based on the standard deviation. As an example, the ABC Company is testing potential job applicants. The average grade on the test given to 25 applicants is 80 (out of 100 points). The standard deviation, when calculated, is 6 points. Thus, one standard deviation (plus or minus) from the mean is 80, plus or minus 6, giving a range from 74 to 86. The normal distribution's properties show

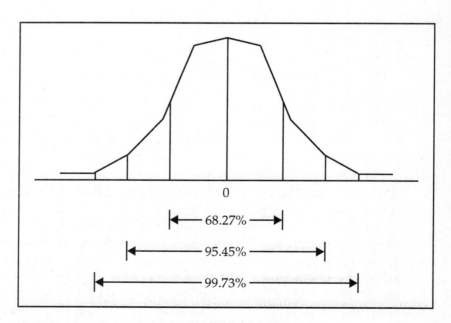

Fig 6.4   Graph of a normal distribution

that approximately 68 per cent of applicants (or 17 individuals) fall into this range. Two standard deviations from the mean gives a range of 68 to 92 (80 plus or minus 12) and includes approximately 95 per cent of applicants. Three standard deviations include 99.7 per cent for a range from 62 to 98.

Normal distributions are used by the aerospace, automotive, construction, information systems, lumber, manufacturing, and pharmaceuticals industries today. And many other industries use normal distributions to identify control limits.

Probability

Defining probability is difficult. Classical definitions include terms such as 'equally likely' or 'equally probable' for the ways that events can happen. Such definitions are misleading because the definition itself uses the term. Although probability is defined statistically, difficulties arise when defining it mathematically (based on relative frequencies, limits, and increasing number of observations to infinity). For simplicity, modern probability theory views the term 'probability' as an undefined concept, similar to a 'point' or 'line' in geometry.

Section 3 Techniques

The techniques used in risk analysis can be expressed for our purposes as a list of four (see Figure 6.5). We will examine each of these later but first, six factors should be kept in mind when conducting risk analysis.

```
●  Three-point estimate
●  Decision tree
●  Monte Carlo simulation
●  Heuristics
```

Fig 6.5   List of techniques for risk analysis

Techniques	Strengths	Weakness
Three-point estimate	• Easy to use • Quick to calculate	• Subjective; dependent on skill of the estimator • May not have historical database to call from • May prove erroneous due to spread between optimistic and pessimistic times
Decision tree	• Attaches probabilities to different outcomes • Decisions are made in stages • Sequence of occurrences can be mapped out like the branches of a tree • Final decision depends on preceding decisions	• Can be incomplete if some parameters are not included in the tree • Can become complex and difficult to diagram if the number of occurrences are high
Monte Carlo simulation technique	• Computer simulation • Use when formal mathematical analysis is not available • Full-scale simulation is worthwhile for large, expensive projects	• Is not an optimizing procedure • A solution is run, not solved • Input is usually generated by random numbers
Heuristics	• Rule of thumb • Hones in on acceptable solution • Use when formal mathematical analysis is not available	• Does not guarantee optimal solution • Results based on subjectivity, i.e., correctness of rule of thumb

Fig 6.6 Strengths and weaknesses of common techniques

1. No technique is perfect. Each has strengths and weaknesses (see Figure 6.6).
2. Some tools and techniques are easier to apply than others. Some require elaborate calculations while others rely on qualitative approaches; for example, judgement based upon a specific characteristic. Some use a combination of both.
3. More detail does not necessarily mean more accuracy or reliability. Analysing risk is at best shooting at a moving target and anticipating something that might happen. Data in a model can quickly become 'dated' or inaccurate due to changing circumstances.
4. It is impossible to eliminate the influence of the analyser. Some level of subjectivity will creep into the analysis, so one must be aware of potential bias and try to avoid or mitigate its effects. A good practice is to identify the assumptions behind the analysis and obtain agreement on them.
5. Risk deals with exposure and uncertainty. Exposure occurs when a risk makes something vulnerable. Different levels of this vulnerability manifest themselves in the form of impacts. What complicates their situation is the level of uncertainty of the risk occurring and its impact.
6. Risk is variable. At any time, the probability of risk and degree of its impact can change. That's because the environment can change for many reasons.

We now look at each of the four techniques in more detail.

Three-point estimate

This technique displays three variables: optimistic, pessimistic, and most likely. They are the basis to calculate the expected values. For example, a schedule slippage occurs. The project manager's job is to estimate the time required to bring the project back on track. The three-point estimate is well suited to this task. An optimistic duration is 4 weeks; pessimistic 25 weeks; and most likely 10 weeks. To calculate the expected duration, the general formula is: [optimistic + (4 × most likely) + pessimistic]/6 yields the answer. Substituting in the values results in: [4 + (4 × 10) + 25]/6 = 11.33 weeks. The result is the expected duration to bring the schedule back on track based on the schedule slippage. However, the spread between optimistic and pessimistic times is so wide that risk reservations must be incorporated when using the 'expected time' calculation.

The formula for the three-point estimate (for calculating time durations) follows a beta probability distribution and falls within the + and –3 standard deviations. This means that 99.73 per cent of the time, the estimate is acceptable.

Decision tree

Occurrences with a finite number of outcomes and given probabilities are called 'stochastic processes'. A tree diagram is used to describe these processes and in computing the probability of an occurrence. To illustrate this we can analyse a schedule slippage of activities on the critical path. The critical path is shown in Figure 6.7.

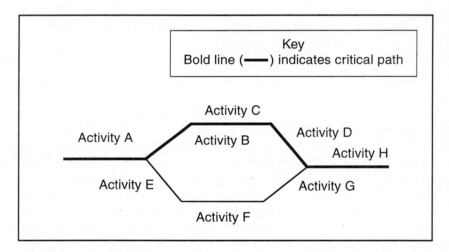

Fig 6.7   Network drawing

Three activities may slide. Activity A has a 50 per cent chance of sliding, Activity B has a 30 per cent chance, and Activity C has a 20 per cent chance (see Figure 6.8). Correcting this situation requires additional resources at a cost of US$600 for Activity A, US$800 for Activity B, and US$2,500 for Activity C. The project manager must determine how much funding to set aside to account for these schedule slippages.

The general formula to determine expected values from the decision tree is: (probability of occurrence) × (output). For this situation, it is the (probability of occurrence) × (cost of fix) for each activity.

- Activity A is (0.50) × (US$600)   = US$ 300
- Activity B is (0.30) × (US$800)   = US$ 240
- Activity C is (0.20) × (US$2,500) = US$ 500
  Total   = US$1,040

Thus, US$1,040 is the budget set aside for potential schedule slippages.

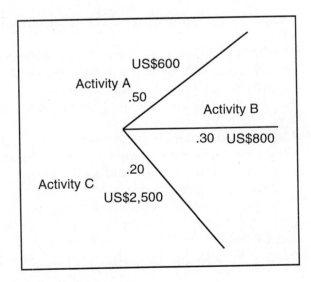

Fig 6.8   Decision tree diagram

Monte Carlo simulation

In this simulation the computer randomly chooses a value from each appropriate probability distribution and combines it with other factors. It assumes that probability distributions can be assigned to the factors of interest, for example, cost and revenue factors like operations, materials, equipment, labour, and research.

The following case study again uses the ABC Company. The company wins the bid to provide heating oil for the winter season to a high-growth rural community. A task team is assigned to determine the optimum number of barrels to store. The project manager must give the executive committee an answer within one week. He feels the Monte Carlo simulation is the necessary tool for the task as it will perform the following ten steps:

1. Identify significant variables.
2. Determine the measure of effectiveness for all variables (listed in Step 1 of the technique) for the system under review.
3. Graph the cumulative probability distribution for each variable.
4. Determine the boundaries or range of random numbers for each variable which directly corresponds with their cumulative probability distribution.
5. Review the data and identify possible solutions to the problem.
6. Use a random number table to generate random numbers.
7. Determine the values of the variables by using the random numbers and the corresponding cumulative probability distribution for each variable.
8. Take the result of Step 7 and substitute it in Step 2 to compute the value of the measure of effectiveness.
9. Repeat Steps 6 to 8 for each solution identified in Step 5.
10. Make a decision based on the results of Step 9.

Ten steps explained
Note that the Monte Carlo simulation uses sample trials performed against a baseline model. The mean value for the measure of effectiveness is determined from a set of sample results for each solution identified in Step 5. Since the means are sample (not population) means, confidence intervals for the true means are calculated by other statistical methods, for example, approximation of sample to population means. What follows is the application of the ten steps to our example of the ABC Company supplying oil to a growing rural community.

Step 1. Identify significant variables
The significant variables include population growth, equipment, insurance premiums, labour, inventory, and usage factors. The amount of oil used is uncertain because the length of the season is variable as is quantity consumed over time. If the ABC Company stores too much oil it will incur unnecessary storage costs. If too little, then additional oil must be imported via freighter, an expensive procedure. The significant variables are the average demand of oil (in barrels) and the length of the winter season.

Step 2. Determine the measure of effectiveness for all variables for the system under review
Two cost measures of effectiveness are formulated. The first costs expression is when the inventory-on-hand is less than or equal to demand:

Total cost = [(cost/barrel of oil on-hand) × (number of barrels of oil on-hand)] + [(cost/barrel of oil on-hand) × (additional barrels required)]

The second cost expression is when the inventory-on-hand is greater than demand:

Total cost = [(cost/barrel of oil on-hand) × (number of barrels of oil on-hand)] + [(holding cost/barrel of oil) × (additional number of barrels required)] or in symbols: when inventory is less than or equal to demand:

Total cost = $(c \times i) + (f \times d) - (f \times I) = ci + f(d-i)$

and when inventory is greater than demand:

Total cost = $(c \times i) + (h \times i) - (h \times d) = ci + h(i-d)$

Demand of barrels of oil (use per week)	Probability	Cumulative probability
250	0.00	0.00
275	0.02	0.02
300	0.20	0.22
325	0.15	0.37
350	0.09	0.46
375	0.04	0.50
400	0.24	0.74
425	0.06	0.80
450	0.01	0.81
475	0.05	0.86
500	0.11	0.97
525	0.03	1.00

Fig 6.9   Demand of oil

where:

i = inventory on hand at the beginning of the season
f = transportation cost for a barrel of oil by freighter = US$10
h = holding cost for a barrel of oil for the winter season = US$3
d = demand for oil for the winter season = (number of weeks in
      the winter season) × (the average demand of oil per week)
c = cost/barrel of oil for inventory-on-hand (which is delivered
      by truck) = US$4

Step 3. Graph the cumulative probability distribution for each variable

The ABC Company maintains a database on both oil demand and weeks in the winter season for its customer base. Capitalizing on this data, tables (see Figures 6.9 and 6.10) are built and subsequent cumulative probability charts (see Figures 6.11 and 6.12) are plotted.

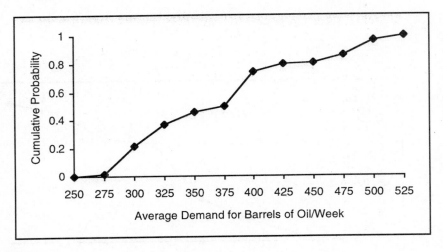

Fig 6.10 Demand for barrels of oil/week

Weeks in winter season	Probability	Cumulative probability
12	0.00	0.00
13	0.05	0.05
14	0.10	0.15
15	0.15	0.30
16	0.40	0.70
17	0.03	0.73
18	0.20	0.93
19	0.07	1.00

Fig 6.11   Weeks in winter season

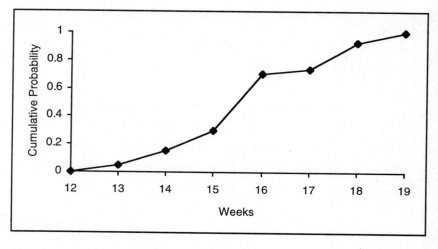

Fig 6.12   Graph of weeks in winter season

***Step 4. Determine the boundaries or range of random numbers
for each variable which directly corresponds with their
cumulative probability distribution***

The assignment of random numbers for each significant variable appears in Figures 6.13 and 6.14. The random numbers for each significant variable are based on its probability. For example, the probability for 275 barrels of oil used/week is 0.02, which translates into two numbers, for example, 0.00 and 0.01. For 300 barrels/week the probability is 0.20, so 20 numbers are used, and so on.

Random numbers	Average demand for barrels of oil/week
00–01	275
02–21	300
22–36	325
37–45	350
46–49	375
50–73	400
74–79	425
80	450
81–85	475
86–96	500
97–99	525

Fig 6.13   Random numbers assigned to demand

Random numbers	Average demand for barrels of oil/week
00–04	13
05–14	14
15–29	15
30–69	16
70–72	17
73–92	18
93–99	19

Fig 6.14   Random numbers assigned to weeks in the season

Step 5. Review the data and identify possible solutions to the problem

A possible solution is that the expected average demand is derived by multiplying the *probability* of the number of barrels consumed weekly by the number of barrels consumed weekly and then adding the products. In this case, the probability of 250 barrels of oil consumed weekly is zero; 275 barrels weekly is 2 per cent, etc. is:

$(0\% \times 250) + (2\% \times 275) + (20\% \times 300) + (15\% \times 325) + (9\% \times 350) + (4\% \times 375) + (24\% \times 400) + (6\% \times 425) + (1\% \times 450) + (5\% \times 475) + (11\% \times 500) + (3\% \times 525) = 381.25$ which is the expected number of barrels consumed weekly.

The same notion applies in determining the expected number of weeks during the winter season:

(0% × 12) + (5% × 13) + (10% × 14) + (15% × 15) + (40% × 16) + (3% × 17) = (20% × 18) = (7% × 19) = 16.14 which is the expected number of weeks during the winter season.

The expected demand for oil in the winter is the product of the expected number of barrels consumed weekly times the expected number of winter weeks or (381.25 × 16.14) = 6,153 barrels demanded. Thus, the project manager can reasonably estimate that the inventory for oil could include 5,900; 6,100; 6,300; 6,500; and 6,700 barrels.

Step 6. Use a random number table to generate random numbers

Step 7. Determine the values of the variables by using the random numbers and the corresponding cumulative probability distribution for each variable

Step 8. Take the result of Step 7 and substitute it in Step 2 to compute the value of the measure of effectiveness

Step 9: Repeat Steps 6 to 8 for each solution identified in Step 5

Steps 6 to 9 execute the simulation. In the first trial, a number, 44, is generated randomly from a random number table. This number corresponds to the expected consumption of 350 barrels. Another random number, 85, is also generated which corresponds to 18 winter weeks. These results from the simulation yield the consumption, or demand, for the winter season by multiplying 350 by 18, giving 6,300 barrels. See Figure 6.15 for a sample of five trials (these five are relatively small: simulations are usually 25 trials or greater; however, what is covered here is for illustration purposes only.

Step 10. Make a decision based on the results of Step 9.
The decision is based on the optimal solution. A total cost is calculated (the last line in Figure 6.15). The lowest sum is US$187,250 with an inventory of 6,700 barrels. Thus, the aver-

Trial number	Oil demand/week		Weeks in winter		Demand for winter season	Financial analysis (using different inventory levels)				
	Random number	Number of barrels of oil/week	Random number	Number of weeks	Number of barrels of oil/week × number of weeks	5,900	6,100	6,300	6,500	6,700
1	80	450	85	18	8,100	45,600	44,400	43,200	42,000	40,800
2	98	525	50	16	8,400	48,600	47,400	46,200	45,000	43,800
3	60	400	95	19	7,600	40,600	39,400	38,200	37,000	35,800
4	90	500	27	15	7,500	39,600	38,400	37,200	36,000	34,800
5	75	425	71	17	7,225	36,850	35,650	34,450	33,250	32,050
					Total cost	211,250	205,250	199,250	193,250	187,250
		Average seasonal cost for 5 trials = Total cost/5				42,250	41,050	39,850	38,650	37,450

Note: Since all demands for the winter season exceeded the expected demand (6,153), the formula used in the financial analysis is the first measure of effectiveness where the inventory-on-hand is less than demand.

Fig 6.15 Monte Carlo simulation. A sample of five trials

age expected winter season cost is US$187,250 per five trials = US$37,450 for the optimal solution. Note that the difference between the optimal solution and the inventory of 6,500 barrels at a cost of US$193,50 is a modest difference. It would be advantageous to run this simulation in more than five trials to obtain a more significant difference. Also, note that the project manager uses only the first measure of effectiveness to calculate the financial costs because the inventory is less than demand. When the inventory is greater than demand, the project manager uses the second measure of effectiveness.

Keep in mind the following thoughts concerning the Monte Carlo simulation used in the above example. The basis for the solution is inventory since total cost depends on it. Total cost of inventory depends on two parameters – holding costs and transportation costs. As holding costs increase, transportation costs decrease – and *vice versa*. In today's just-in-time environment – whether construction, information systems, pharmaceuticals – companies find it advantageous to minimize inventory and capitalize on long-term relationships with suppliers.[1] The optimal solution for this example is the one with an inventory level that minimizes the summation of holding and transportation costs.

The optimal solution of 6,700 barrels at a cost of US$37,450 is not the expected demand level of 6,100 (rounded from 6,153) at a cost of US$41,050. A sensitivity analysis occurs for inventory levels above and below 6,700 barrels. Also, additional trials should occur to obtain more reliable results. Another approach might be to perform sensitivity analysis on the probability distributions and then perform the financial analysis to determine a different optimal solution.

Heuristics

Heuristics means 'rule of thumb'. People develop their own rule of thumb based on their experiences acquired over the years. Heuristics has been used over the millennia to estimate, calculate, uncover, discover, purify, and simplify solutions to problems. Rarely are algorithms attached to heuristics; however, this approach is better than unstructured and random ones. Heuristics also does not guarantee developing an optimal solution. The main idea is to progress, not to be perfect. Moving towards a suitable solution is forward advancement. Again, heuristics is generally used when no specificity exists and no alternatives are recognizable.

Precedence diagramming method

The precedence diagramming method (PDM) for risk analysis is a technique that takes an ordinal approach for determining priorities.[2] This prioritization reflects the ranking of a set of variables by importance according to some criteria.

One or more individuals conduct the ranking. Although involving some mathematics, it is mainly a qualitative technique using the judgement of one or more individuals.

This technique offers four advantages over the previous techniques discussed in this chapter.

1. It is simple to use. The other techniques, with the exception of the decision tree, require considerable calculation.
2. Because of its simplicity, it requires less time to perform. It also requires less effort and knowledge to complete it.
3. It is highly flexible in its application. Project managers can use it to define multiple priorities, not just financial ones.
4. The results are easily understood. Once completed by project managers, everyone on the project can reference it.

Fig 6.16   Identify components

	Roof	Frame	Foundation	Plumbing	
Roof					0 + 6 = 6 Third priority
Frame 2	3				2 + 7.5 = 9.5 First priority
Foundation 3	2	5			3 + 2.5 = 5.5 Fourth priority
Plumbing 4	1	2.5	2.5	2.5	9 + 0 = 9 Second priority
	6	7.5	2.5		

Fig 6.17 Rank components

83

In applying PDM, we can identify six steps.

1. Identify the components of the subject (for example, system, product) being studied (see Figure 6.16).
2. Rank the components according to some criteria. The ranking reflects descending importance (see Figure 6.17).
3. Identify the risks or goals to the components of the subject being studied (see Figure 6.18).

Fig 6.18   Identify risks or goals

4. Rank the risks or goals according to some criteria. The ranking reflects descending importance (see Figure 6.19).
5. Complete each cell, built by the intersection of a component and a risk or goal (see Figure 6.20). The cell might include controls to prevent or mitigate risks or the results of an evaluation scheme.

Conclusion

Each technique has its strengths and weaknesses. The requirement here is to choose one that will meet requirements, is easy to learn, and analyses the risks reliably and accurately. In short, the chosen technique depends on how well the risk assessment is carried out.

Table — Rank risks or goals (paired comparison):

	Rain	Snow	Hail	Frost
Rain		4	2	1
Snow	1		2	0
Hail	3	3		1
Frost	4	5	4	
	7	2		1

Snow: 0 + 7 = 7 Third priority

Hail: 2 + 1 = 3 Fourth priority

1 + 6 = 7 Second priority

Frost: 13 + 0 = 13 First priority

Fig 6.19 Rank risks or goals

Threat / Component	Frost	Hail	Rain	Snow
Frame	None	None	Varnish	Varnish
Plumbing	Padding	None	None	Padding
Roof	Shingles	Shingles	Tar	Tar
Foundation	None	None	Sump pump	None

Fig 6.20   Complete each cell

7   Step Three: Risk Control

Risk control is the third step of the risk management cycle. Its purpose is to handle risks in a manner that achieves project goals efficiently and effectively.

Break with the past

Under traditional risk management, there are four ways of handling risk:

- Acceptance
- Adoption
- Avoidance
- Transfer

Acceptance
When a risk arises, project managers decide to let the risk occur by taking no action. In other words, they are willing to accept the consequence. For example, a task on the critical path slips,

extending the project completion date. The project manager does nothing.

Adoption
When a risk arises, project managers coexist with it. They may not like the risk but accept it. They take some action to manage its effects. For example, a project's budget is cut by 30 per cent. The project manager reduces expenditures on training and overtime to compensate for the reduction.

Avoidance
Project managers take action to avoid one or more risks. For example, a project manager may produce a schedule to avoid the possibility of missing well-publicized critical milestones.

Transfer
Project managers share risks, such as with another project or a consultant. For example, the completion of a particular deliverable depends on the actions and impacts of two projects. Failure to develop the desired item results in a penalty that both projects must share.

The aforementioned breakdown of handling risks is tactical rather than strategic. It encourages responding to risks in ways that are frequently 'quick fixes' and incremental in scale. Risk acceptance, adoption, avoidance, and transfer are immediate responses to the current moment but are not the sources of the problem. The approach is highly reactive. Thus, risk reaction typically manifests itself by:

- Adding more people, equipment, supplies, and money
- Addressing immediate concerns
- Changing team leadership and membership
- Concentrating on re-planning for the moment, ignoring long-term consequences
- Handling the project in an isolated manner
- Having too much or too little flexibility
- Performing quick fixes

Effective project managers must face up to the fundamental issues surrounding risks rather than applying and re-applying bandaids. The successful course of action is that of implementing the right project management process to the right degree. The project accomplishes its goals and objectives efficiently and effectively with the least risk. Such an approach is called risk 'pro-action'.

Risk pro-action

Risk pro-action ensures that appropriate project management processes are in place to handle risks efficiently and effectively. This is achieved by establishing appropriate processes before a project progresses too far. The further into its life cycle a project progresses the more costly it is to address a risk (see Figure 7.1). This is especially the case where the origin of a risk was in an earlier phase. The impact of a risk manifests itself in the form of cost, schedule, and quality. Hence, having the right processes in place enables efficient and effective project management.

As the life cycle progresses, the more costly it is to address risks.

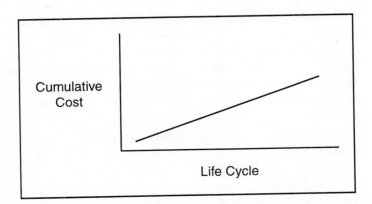

Fig 7.1   Cost impact of a risk

There are six interrelated ways to achieve efficient and effective project management while reducing the number and impact of risks on projects.

- Using an effective early warning system
- Adopting a project management methodology
- Performing contingency planning
- Reusing components
- Improving processes
- Training

Using an effective warning system

A good first step that project managers can take to manage risk is to establish a monitoring or early warning system, efficient enough to detect deviations from plans and to continuously monitor performance.

Project managers should base this early warning system on identifying variance: that is, the difference between what was planned and what has occurred. Two prime areas for such a system are schedule and cost.

When a deviation occurs between planned and actual a possibility exists that a project is facing an uncontrolled risk. A variance may be positive or negative. For example, the difference between a planned late finish date and an actual finish date for a task may indicate an ahead of or a behind schedule circumstance. The former situation is often positive; the latter negative, although not necessarily. Hence, differences between schedule dates is one deviation an early warning system will detect.

Another early warning system regarding schedules is to look at float, or slack. Float is the time an activity can slip in the schedule before impacting the critical path. Typically, the critical path, which is the longest path in a network diagram, has very little float. The more float decreases during a project the greater the likelihood that a risk has impacted. The lower the float the more critical the task.

The difference between budgeted and actual expenditures must be monitored. A variance between the two indicates too little or too much spending for the work completed. The former situation is often positive; the latter negative, although not necessarily.

Ideally, project managers want a way to monitor project progress and determine whether a risk has a big impact. Earned value helps them accomplish that.

Earned value involves reviewing schedule and budget performance together by looking at three variables: budgeted cost for work scheduled (BCWS); budgeted cost of work performed (BCWP); and actual cost of work performed (ACWP).

These three variables help project managers determine how well cost and schedule performance vary from plans. BCWS is the cost targeted to complete if following the project plan. BCWP is the value of the work completed up to a specific point in time; it is also known as earned value. ACWP is the amount spent to complete work up to a specific point in time. BCWS, BCWP, and ACWP exist for each task and the entire project.

Using all three variables, project managers can calculate the variance to cost and schedule. They can calculate cost variances with this formula:

Cost variance = BCWP – ACWP

They can also calculate schedule variance with this formula:

Schedule variance = BCWP – BCWS

If the value they calculate for one or both is negative, then project managers need to analyse and evaluate the cause. Negative numbers indicate potentially negative situations and project managers should identify cause and circumstance. The best place to identify these is to first look at tasks on the critical path. These tasks are affected by most risks.

Adopting a project management methodology

Most surveys on project management reveal less than satisfactory results regarding project management process implementation. Many projects lack adequate support, complete plans, sub-contracting detail, and have unclear goals. These and other deficiencies increase the likelihood of project failure rather than success. Not surprisingly, the risks and their impacts are high.

A project management methodology can help avoid or alleviate those risks that cause such dismal results. The purpose of such a methodology is to provide guidelines and instructions for leading, defining, planning, organizing, controlling, and closing projects efficiently and effectively (see Figure 7.2).

A methodology provides several benefits.

- It provides a standardized approach for managing projects. With greater standardization comes less confusion because participants in the project communicate on the same 'wavelength'. People can identify and respond to risks with less confusion.
- It improves communications, a concomitant of standardization. People use the same jargon, forms, and reports when working on a project. Better communications allows greater sharing of information which, in turn, leads to improved ways to identify risks and respond to them.
- It enables project managers to respond more effectively to changing conditions because the methodology provides the necessary guidelines and instructions. Following the guidelines and instructions and even tailoring them when dealing with risk does not mean rigidity or fluidity. It means adaptability, flexibility. Methodology is a 'living' tool.
- It provides better expectations of results. Implementing processes in the manner described in a methodology gives participants some reasonable expectations of what the results might be. From a risk perspective, it means consistency towards managing risk via a standardized application of project management processes.
- It results in greater productivity. Standardization, better re-

LEADING	<ul><li>Communicating</li><li>Maintaining direction</li><li>Motivating</li><li>Support</li><li>Team-building</li><li>Vision</li></ul>
DEFINING	<ul><li>Project announcement</li><li>Statement of work</li></ul>
PLANNING	<ul><li>Cost calculation</li><li>Estimating</li><li>Resource allocation</li><li>Risk control</li><li>Schedules</li><li>Work breakdown structure</li></ul>
ORGANIZING	<ul><li>Automated tools</li><li>Forms</li><li>History files</li><li>Library</li><li>Memos</li><li>Newsletters</li><li>Procedures</li><li>Project manual</li><li>Project office</li><li>Reports</li><li>Team organization</li><li>Workflows</li></ul>
CONTROLLING	<ul><li>Change control</li><li>Contingency planning</li><li>Corrective action</li><li>Meetings</li><li>Replanning</li><li>Status collection and assessment</li></ul>
CLOSING	<ul><li>Lessons learned</li><li>Post-implementation review</li><li>Statistical compilation</li><li>Winding-down activities</li></ul>

Fig 7.2   Contents of a typical project management methodology

sponsiveness, improved communications, and reasonable expectations mean less complexity, confusion, and conflict on projects. That, in turn, reduces opportunities for external and self-induced risks from occurring or having a significant impact on project results.

To realize these benefits, of course, a methodology must have several characteristics and conditions. It contains sufficient coverage of the six processes of project management: leading, defining, planning, organizing, controlling, and closing. The content is comprehensive enough to prove meaningful to users yet not so inundated with detail that it constrains a project when responding to different situations.

A methodology provides the rudimentary basics for each project management topic: who, what, when, where, why, and how. Such basic information is necessary to respond adequately under varying circumstances.

Users must accept the methodology. They must see it as a useful tool for planning and managing projects. Above all, they must view it as a tool to manage risk, giving them the guidelines and instructions to take efficient and effective action.

Closely linked to acceptance is compliance. Users must comply with the contents; they must and should use the contents to varying degrees to manage projects in general and for risk specifically. A methodology serves absolutely no purpose unless people use it.

A methodology contains ample graphics and examples. Graphics not only replace text but also communicate information quickly and, in turn, enable users to process information rapidly. The graphics must contain real-life examples and the more the better. Users can borrow and adapt those examples for their own projects.

In the same vein, a methodology also contains templates of documents that users can apply when managing projects. These templates, often stored on a computing platform, can be directly applied to any given circumstances. For example, templates for building oral or written risk reports and blank copies of forms to be completed in a standardized way.

Guidelines and instructions for managing projects, to include handling certain risk scenarios, are part of the methodology. These guidelines and instructions are modular and scaleable so that users can adapt them to their environment.

There should be some criteria in the design of a methodology to assess the quality of processes being implemented and deliverables produced. For example, some criteria to assess the quality of a risk management plan.

A methodology should – like any other business document – be easy to follow and concise. Users must be able to find what they need when they need it.

Finally, a methodology encompasses the processes of project management: for leading, it discusses topics like motivation and communication; for defining, topics like statement of work; for planning, topics like work breakdown structure; for organizing, topics like automated tools; for controlling, topics like status collection; and for closing, topics like post-implementation review.

Performing contingency planning

Project managers must, for effectiveness and efficiency, plan for the immediate and distant future. Conducting a thorough risk identification and analysis that identifies the types of risks that could occur, their priority, and their impact is essential. However, possession of the information for its own sake is meaningless; the information must be applied to manage risks, as and when they arise. Contingency planning is the best method to achieve this goal.

Contingency planning is preparing oneself to handle a given circumstance that may arise in the future – for example, an external risk, such as reduction of a project's budget by 20 per cent.

A good contingency plan, therefore, views a risk as being caused by something – a 'trigger'. In other words, a cause–effect relationship exists. Just accepting a risk and not addressing the cause only encourages reactive, not proactive, project manage-

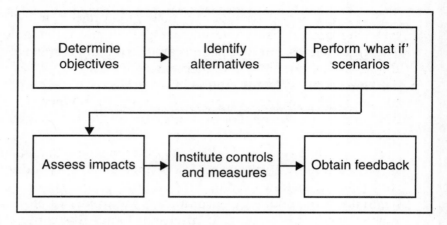

Fig 7.3   Flowchart for a contingency plan

ment. The plan should identify the cause. A sample flowchart for a contingency plan is shown in Figure 7.3 and in Figure 7.4 an overview of triggers for risk cause and effect.

Project managers should conduct, at a minimum, contingency plans for tasks on the critical path of a schedule. Such tasks, if missing their start or stop dates or both, impact the completion date for the entire project.

A contingency plan contains a description of a risk, any assumptions used to develop the plan, the probability of a risk occurring, its impact, and the appropriate response. Figure 7.5 is an example of a form used to perform contingency planning for critical tasks and other circumstances.

Frequently, risks arise that were unanticipated. Logically, contingency planning doesn't make sense because the event has already occurred. Under such circumstances, an action item log, like the one shown in Figure 7.6, may prove useful. It contains a description of the risk, its priority (critical, non-critical), its impact (low, medium, high), the person responsible for managing the risk, and the date when handling the risk will be complete.

Triggers of cause	Effect
Cultural/societal	Societal view and opinion
Economic	Cost of failure
Human	Life threatening
Labour	Strikes
Legal	Judicial system and enforcement; government policies
Managerial	Organizational direction
Market	Market share/penetration
Media	Public support
Moral	Spiritual perspective
Political	Status
Technical	Impact of 'it can't be done now'

Fig 7.4　Triggers of cause and effect

Reusing components

The term simply means the using of pieces or parts of a system, product, or project to solve a problem or achieve a goal. Component reuse is frequently associated with software and hardware. Yet, reuse can occur for other items, too (see Figure 7.7).[1]

In project management estimates, work breakdown structures, schedules, and documentation that have been used and tested on previous projects of a similar nature can all be reused. The

Risk description
Assumptions
Probability
Circle one: High   Medium   Low
Impact Technical: Operational: Functional:
Response

Fig 7.5   Contingency plan

Task no.	Risk description	Priority	Impact	Responsibility	Estimated resolution date	Actual completion date

Fig 7.6 Action item log

99

1.	Specifications	7.	Implementations
2.	Design	8.	Data
3.	Code	9.	Databases
4.	Test suites	10.	Tools
5.	Standards	11.	Documentation
6.	Interfaces	12.	Templates

Fig 7.7   Twelve types of components to enter the reuse library

concept and application of reuse is valuable in managing risk because project managers can apply items of substantial similarity, such as data and responses, to specific risk situations.

Reuse is applicable, also, to components – previously tested for defects through experience – that are reliable, defect free, and require minimum subsequent testing even after some modification. Such components improve project performance, reducing approvals, cycle time, delays, inspections, inventories, lead times, overtime, rework loops, and set-up activities. The bottom line is that reuse of components enables project managers to handle risks, especially critical ones, quickly and effectively without struggling with administrative complexities or operating in confusion.

When a component is reused it should have several characteristics. It should be modular, that is, have definable boundaries that distinguish it from other components. It should be unifunctional, that is, perform one function or for groups of modules doing related functions. It can consist of several smaller modules that perform a subset of a higher function. Hence, a component could be a 'super' module that consists of smaller modules performing related functions. No optimum size for a component exists because, in theory, a component may be an entire system or a subset of a larger one.

What is required for component reuse to work? The answer is to establish a reuse library, enabling an organization to store and retrieve components and share them among projects.

1. Is the component reusable? Does it perform more stand-alone operations, or does it have potential to be reused within a given system or across multiple systems?

2. Does the component meet customer needs? Does its functionality, environment, or structure meet our requirements?

3. Has the component passed our test criteria? Has the component been successfully reused a pre-specified number of times? If so, freeze the component and enter it into the reuse library, otherwise, keep it available until it can be frozen.

4. Does the component meet with the competition? Is it better technically? Is it a better value to enter it into the reuse library than to make it non-reusable? Is it easy to maintain? Is it cost-effective to maintain?

5. Are total costs minimized, including infrastructure costs for the library? Infrastructure costs include security, configuration control, problem tracking, project management, and quality control.

6. What is the warranty policy for the component? What is the component's life expectancy after it is placed in the library? What are the plans for retiring the component?

Fig 7.8 Sample criteria for components to enter the library

Figure 7.8 provides some criteria for determining what components can enter a library.[2]

Improving processes

Improving processes, particularly those of project management, enables project managers to respond more efficiently and effectively to high-risk situations.

Process improvement for projects offers many benefits. Projects proceed more efficiently with streamlined processes and thereby ensure a greater chance of meeting client requirements. Participants experience less frustration and more involvement. Finally, projects operate at greater productivity levels which, in turn, increase profitability.

Process improvement for projects is brought about through:

● Continuous quality improvement
● Business process re-engineering
● Benchmarking

Continuous quality improvement

Commonly known as CQI, continuous quality improvement seeks incremental change to project management processes. Areas to improve are highlighted by collecting data, identifying variances, receiving customer feedback, and recognizing individuals who improve processes. These activities occur according to the Deming cycle of plan, do, check, and act (see Chapter

---

● Encourage widespread participation
● Follow the Deming cycle (plan, do, check, act)
● Identify the key areas
● Look at both normalities and abnormalities
● Receive and integrate customer feedback into processes
● Recognize and reward efforts and innovations
● Stress 'continuous' in CQI
● Support analysis with facts and data
● Use standard tools

Fig 7.9   Necessary considerations for applying CQI

1). Some common tools of CQI tools include Pareto diagrams, scatter diagrams, flowcharting, and frequency analysis.

CQI works best when the environment is fairly stable and improvement can occur incrementally. By improving project processes, project managers concentrate more on managing risk without fear of being hamstrung by administrative bottlenecks. It also allows them to understand their key processes for better managing their projects. Figure 7.9 lists the necessary considerations for successfully applying CQI efforts on projects.

Business process re-engineering

Commonly known as BPR, business process re-engineering involves, unlike CQI, completely overhauling or replacing processes. To accomplish such radical transformation two techniques are employed: modelling tools and workflow software.

Modelling tools are diagrams identifying objects and activities in a process flow and illustrating how they interact with one another. Specific information documented for existing and proposed processes are data, people, technology, business rules, activities, policies, procedures, and physical infrastructure.

Workflow software helps to capture and compare existing and proposed processes (see Figure 7.10).

Both modelling and workflow tools should answer the basic questions of who, what, when, where, why, and how.

BPR improves the management of projects in general and risks in particular by identifying and removing situations where processes create needless risks or make an effective response difficult, if not impossible. Some opportunities to adopt effective project management processes include reducing complexity in executing processes, simplifying the organizational structure of a project, removing redundancy in executing processes, integrating multiple processes, and even establishing missing processes. Like CQI, the sooner BPR is applied to a project (see Figure 7.11) the greater the impact of the change and less resistance to it. Once projects start it is more difficult to slow the momentum for making any substantive changes to processes without disrupting progress.

- Architectural compliance
- Cost
- Documentation
- Integration with other toolsets
- Modelling techniques support
- Operability
- Portability
- Scaleability
- Training
- Upgradeability
- User-friendliness
- Vendor support
- Warranty

Fig 7.10   Necessary considerations for purchasing a workflow tool

- Apply project management to BPR effort
- Constantly communicate the goals and results
- Designate a process owner
- Focus on vital or 'core' processes
- Concentrate on the customer
- Map processes for a reasonable amount of time
- Obtain management support
- Recognize BPR is a cultural as well as a process change
- Use standardized tools and techniques

Fig 7.11   Necessary considerations for applying BPR

Benchmarking

Used as a process improvement tool, benchmarking compares and adapts processes performed better at another company, preferably a leader in a particular industry.

There are two core benefits offered to project managers. Benchmarking, first, forces project managers, especially those engaged in large projects, to document processes, thereby learning about what they do and don't do well, including risk management. And, second, benchmarking encourages project managers to overcome the 'ostrich syndrome' by encouraging them to look beyond their immediate needs and to identify ways to do business better.

For benchmarking to succeed, a number of actions are mandatory. The project manager must:

1. Assign the right people on the benchmarking team. Pick people with sufficient knowledge and global understanding to benchmark a process. Also ensure that the people have adequate time to do the job correctly.

2. Document the process to be benchmarked. Project managers must know what to compare against before benchmarking other firms. Base documentation upon some criteria to compare 'apples with apples' and not 'apples and oranges' or even 'apples with bowling balls'.

3. When documenting the process ensure that everyone agrees on the modelling techniques and tools to use. Failure to do so will disrupt communications among team members and frustrate everyone when benchmarking occurs.

4. Identify the primary benchmarking activity, avoiding the tendency towards scope grope by benchmarking everything. Concentrate on what's critical.

5. Benchmark during stable times. If a project is under immense pressure, avoid benchmarking because it takes considerable time and effort to conduct research and formulate conclusions.

6. Standardize internal processes as much as possible. If employing a methodology, standardization is present as long as compliance exists. If not, project managers can take steps to make benchmarking easier. They can document their existing processes, especially vital ones. They can also establish qualitative and quantitative metrics to set standards and track progress. Standards and metrics enable comparisons with other companies easier.

7. Consider the behavioural aspects of benchmarking. Many

project members view it as threatening because it may lessen their role or threaten their job security, thereby encouraging their resistance to benchmarking. Project managers should therefore obtain management commitment to benchmark project management processes; explain clearly how everyone will gain from it; and explain clearly how their projects will benefit from it.

Training

Training employees to understand risk is especially important. Trained staff are better prepared to deal with risk proactively than are untrained staff. A training programme will include knowledge, experience, training needs, expectations, and feedback.

Knowledge
Training empowers employees with proper tools to perform their jobs well. Therefore, knowledge is power. Various aspects of training include analytical, legal, political, technological, and interpersonal skills. These aspects give employees a better understanding of risk and, subsequently, how to deal effectively with it.

Experience
The factor which separates the novice from the seasoned professional is experience. Different types of experience include: hands-on training, attitude (for example, emphasizing positive viewpoints), behaviour or actions, motivation, and risk-taking. People are different and so are their experiences. Experience may be passed on from employee to employee via oral (casual talking) and written (documented lessons learned) communication.

Training needs
Depending on the person and the task or assignment required of them, training needs will vary. Relevant coursework must be

determined and appropriate personnel educated to ensure a proper perspective of risk-taking. Necessary classes are scheduled and people dedicate their time to attend these classes. Training allows staff members to 'get up to speed' quickly in vital work areas. The small amount of time and money spent on training team members can reap innumerable benefits.

Expectations

Good project managers have expectations. Expectations can take the form of milestones, such as a deliverable attached to a schedule. However, events do not always happen as planned, so preparation for the unknown is necessary. The better prepared the team is for the unknown, such as having contingency plans in place, the smoother the operation recovers when the 'unlikely' event occurs.

Feedback

Often overlooked in many processes, feedback is the key to process improvement. Good project managers communicate lessons learned and experiences from all parties involved in the risk management process, including customers and suppliers. (Note that in any process, customers can also be users and vice versa.) By keeping communication lines open, feedback is encouraged at all levels within the organization.

Pro-action, not reaction

Embarking on projects is a risky endeavour. Just about anything can happen that can negatively impact results. It is difficult, even impossible, to prepare for every eventuality. Having the right measures in place and improving them constantly are the best ways to ensure that project managers respond to risks, particularly negative ones, efficiently and effectively. Waiting for something to happen and then taking action only encourages reaction rather than pro-action.

8 Step Four: Risk Reporting

The fourth step in the risk management cycle is risk reporting. It provides information on the status of managing risk and prepares the groundwork for effective decision-making.

There are two types of reporting mechanisms employed in risk reporting: written and oral. Project managers may prefer one over the other – or they may use both in different circumstances.

Characteristics of effective risk reports

Regardless of which of the two mechanisms used, risk reports should have several characteristics. These are grouped into three categories: qualitative, content, and display (see Figure 8.1).

Qualitative characteristics
As the name implies, these characteristics address the quality of the risk reports. At a minimum, risk reports should be easy to read and omit clutter and jargon. They should present informa-

• Qualitative	• Content	• Display
– Clarity	– Assumptions	– Audience needs
– Concise	– Background	– Illustrations
– Honest	– Comprehensive	– Overload prevention
– Meaningfulness	– Criticality	
– Objective	– Descriptive	
– Relevancy	– Facts and data	
– Timeliness	– Prescriptive	

Fig 8.1   Risk report categories

tion, not data, be pertinent to the subject, communicate in a straightforward way to the audience, and be free of bias.

Content characteristics

The content of a risk report, of course, is extremely important. Enough information for the audience or readership to effectively decide on a specific issue should be presented, as well as essential assumptions, facts, and data. Content will include enough background to enable readers or listeners to understand what has occurred up to the moment; what are the existing state of circumstances; and what the situation should be. If a variance exists between what is and what should be then the content should include recommendations for improving the situation.

In an earlier work, we assembled a 'Risk Assessment Checklist'.[1] The checklist contains risk considerations for assessing any project (see Figure 8.2).

Display characteristics

As marketing professionals say, 'It's all in the packaging.' While an exaggeration, some truth exists in the statement. When risk reporting, project managers package their reports so readers or the audience can receive, digest, and appreciate information presented to them. To do this they need to understand their audience or readership. If presenting to core team members, project managers usually provide detailed information; if presenting to senior management, they normally present high-level

I. Identify planning risks, related to:
   A. Statement of work
   B. Work breakdown structure
   C. Time estimates
   D. Budget estimates
   E. Scheduling
   F. Product definition
   G. Automated project management
   H. Project plan
   I. Life cycle

II. Identify organizing risks, related to:
   A. Task assignments
   B. Staffing
   C. Training
   D. Project handbook
   E. Reports
   F. Forms
   G. Resource allocation, regarding:
      • People
      • Hardware
      • Software
      • Data
      • Supplies
      • Facilities
   H. Organization chart
   I. Client participation
   J. Senior management support

III. Identify controlling risks related to:
   A. Contingency plans
   B. Tracking of plans versus actuals, like:
      • Cost
      • Schedule
      • Quality
  Meetings like:
      • Status review
      • Checkpoint review
      • Change control
      • Configuration management
      • Quality assurance
      • Milestone benchmarks

IV. Identify technical risks, related to:
   A. Requirements
   B. Design
   C. Tools
   D. Documentation
   E. Quality
   F. Training
   G. Security

Fig 8.2 Risk assessment checklist

information; and if presenting to a client, they will deliver more business rather than technical information.

Regardless, project managers must remember not to provide too much or too little information. Too many details bore senior management and frustrate a client. Too few details cause similar results with core team members. The key is to know the audience and present the information in a form which will be digested easily.

Project managers should use as many illustrations as possible. Confucius was right: a picture is worth a thousand words. One illustration on a page may replace ten written pages. The audience dictates to what extent project managers will use illustrations in their risk reports.

Written report

A written report works best when a permanent record of the assessment is necessary for future use; when people who can't attend need the information; and when time is available to prepare the report itself. A written report is not best when only people with poor writing skills are available; when time is of the essence; and no one will use the report it in the future.

In preparation, the following pitfalls should be avoided as written risk reports often suffer from:

- Typographical errors, sentence fragments, and poor grammar. Reports presented in this way result in the readership not being receptive – no matter how reliable and accurate the facts and data might be. The appearance of the product, while not necessarily reality, gives the appearance of reality. If what's presented looks appealing, readers will be more receptive to the contents and the overall message.
- Unclear or illogical structure; the sequence of the material does not represent clear thinking. Readers must struggle to understand the rationale of the authors. Clarity of thought eases reading and helps readers come to a logical conclusion.

- A lack of facts and data. Instead, risk reports become a repository of opinions, beliefs, assumptions, and attitudes which build walls rather than bridges between author and reader. The reason is that facts and data are difficult to dispute, whereas opinions, beliefs, assumptions, and attitudes are not. When the report is disputed the communications bridge between author and reader collapses easily and quickly.
- Too much verbiage and cluttered diagrams, reflecting the old adage of 'shoving ten pounds of groceries into a five pound bag'. By placing too much information in narratives and illustrations, project managers can create an immediate block in the audience's mind, thereby destroying the bridge once again. In all reporting, present only the essentials; less is best.
- Incomplete or incorrect distribution. People failing to receive reports communicates the mistaken, maybe correct, impression that they don't count. That impression creates a wall but, more importantly, generates resistance towards the information in the report. Resistance to the contents will also arise if individuals who receive a copy acquire information that they're not entitled to, thereby alienating people who have the sole right to know.

A well-written risk report has a basic, modifiable structure the elements of which are:

- Introduction
- Background
- Scope
- Criteria and assumptions
- Approach
- Findings
- Recommendations

Introduction
Describes the purpose of the report, who requested it, who it's for, and its frequency of preparation.

Background
Presents information about the project and the factors initiating its development. It also describes any previous reports.

Scope
Describes what the report does and does not cover: in other words, the parameters of the report. The coverage might include only specific goals, risks, or processes.

Criteria and assumptions
Presents the scheme used to evaluate a project's situation and recommends ways for improvement. It also lists assumptions so readers can better understand the rationale behind the report.

Approach
Describes the risk analysis technique used to derive the conclusions presented in the report. This description is at a high level, avoiding the 'how to's of executing the technique.

Findings
Presents the findings up to the date of the report. These findings typically fall into one or more of the six basic categories of project management; however, they can be grouped in other ways.

Recommendations
If findings present one or more problems, this section describes ways to address them. It's best to present several recommendations and let readers select the best one, thereby avoiding the accusation of being 'forced' to accept an unworkable solution.

Oral report

An alternative or complement to the written report is the oral report.[2] This is best used when an immediate need for information about risk exists; when the time frame to prepare a written report is too short; when the spoken word can communicate important ideas better than a written one; and when no one has the ability to write.

The oral report has all the characteristics of a well-written report and follows the same structure. Like its written counterpart, it frequently suffers from the same shortcomings. The only real difference is that the mode of delivery changes. Project managers must communicate their message before audiences, and how well they deliver their message can determine whether they build bridges or walls.

In a previous work,[3] we identified six elements for giving effective presentations. They are:

- Perspective – knowing yourself and your audience
- Perception   – how you perceive your audience and how your audience perceives you
- Planning   – determining the type and structure of the presentation
- Preparation – developing the material
- Practice   – rehearsing to improve your performance
- Performance – delivering the presentation

Perspective
Analysing yourself and the audience.

Perception
Understanding the physical and emotional relationships between yourself and your audience.

Planning
Answering questions regarding the who, what, when, where, why, and how of a presentation.

Preparation
Structuring the presentation, incorporating content to support ideas, and determining the mode of delivery.

Practice
Developing techniques for rehearsing.

Performance
The delivery of the presentation.

These six elements apply just as much to an oral report on risk management as they do with any type of formal presentation. *Stand and Deliver* provides checklists for preparing presentations that readers can use when giving oral risk reports.

Two key ingredients

Whatever medium they choose to deliver risk reports, project managers must first identify the message and the audience. Armed with such information, they can develop meaningful, accurate reports that keep the right people informed with the right information in the right amount at the right time.

Part III
Risk Management in Action

9 A Case Study

The following case study is derived from an earlier work published in 1994.[1] David Michaels was responsible for dismantling a zoo containing 3,000 animals. The task was to be completed within a specific time-frame and on the understanding that everyone, including himself, would face redundancy if it was not. David Michaels succeeded and now begins a new project.

Background

The Yuggenheim Foundation wants to add a wild animal park, called RAW, *Roaming Animals of the Wilderness*, to the new zoo that was built after the Zoo Dismantling Project had been completed by David Michaels (see Figure 9.1). Craig Yuggenheim, the Foundation's chief executive, wants David to manage the RAW project. The Foundation expects to generate approximately US$150 million a year in net revenue from the park. However, the Foundation cannot use any of the resources or revenue of the adjacent zoo. To do so would invite tax problems and the Yuggenheim Foundation may loose its tax exempt status.

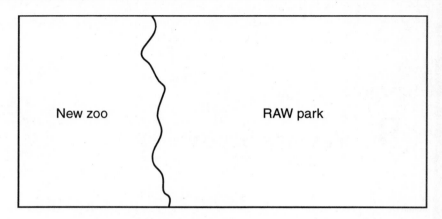

Fig 9.1   RAW park annexe to new zoo

Scope

Before construction begins, Craig Yuggenheim wants to see a risk management plan consisting of risk management, risk analysis, risk control, and risk reporting.

Craig Yuggenheim noted four goals for the project:

- Provide high publicity for the project
- Complete the project on schedule
- Keep construction costs within budget
- Retain a 75 per cent exotic animals ratio

The Yuggenheim Foundation believes in keeping its overheads low. Instead of investing in huge amounts of equipment and inventories, it takes a just-in-time approach. Hence, it leases machinery and keeps on hand minimum levels of materials, supplies, and tools. A general contractor provides machinery (for example, backhoes and forklifts), materials (lumber and fencing), supplies (nails and screws), and tools (hammers and drill bits). Equipment, materials, supplies, and tools are provided at no cost to the RAW project; the Foundation has arranged a special agreement with the general contractor. The only cost the project faces is for permanent and contract labour.

Description of RAW

The site reserved for RAW will not be more than 640,000 acres and will contain herbivores and carnivores. Animals are expected to have as much freedom as possible to roam without endangering others and the grounds should be designed to resemble their habitat as closely as possible.

Mr Yuggenheim expects the park to have at least the following facilities (see Figure 9.2):

- Administrative office
- Food center
- Medical center
- Outdoor stage for special events
- Parking lot
- RAW gift store
- Restrooms
- Veterinary care center

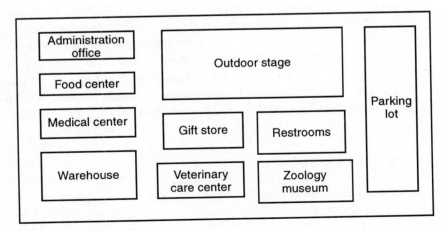

Fig 9.2 RAW facilities

- Warehouse
- Zoology museum

Project constraints

Schedule
The project must begin on 30 January 19XX, and must finish not later than 4 November. Management has mandated that David Michaels must meet the end date without exception. The 40-hour week starts at 8.00a.m. on Monday and finishes at 4.30p.m. on Friday. Each employee is entitled to a 30-minute lunch break and two 10-minute breaks with one in the morning and one in the afternoon. Management does not allow working on the weekends and operations continue during holidays at double-time rates of pay.

Budget
The project cannot exceed US$700,000. Project costs consist of labour only.

Resource
Several people are to support the project. Being a cross-functional or matrix environment, these people may or may not support multiple projects. Although management has given RAW top priority, the middle management politics are so severe that David Michaels may not have some staff members available when he needs them. If he temporarily doesn't use a person to some degree, he may lose them, permanently.

The assessment

David Michaels knew that project management at the Yuggenheim Foundation had a history of mixed results, leaning more on the negative side. Projects frequently exceeded costs, had inadequate schedule performance, resulted in poor quality, and eventually demotivated project participants, especially core team members.

He looked at several risk identification and analysis techniques. He wanted a technique that: pinpointed those processes which are essential to achieve project goals; provided an objective review of a project as it currently exists; one that monitored improving project management processes; provided warning signs before problems in the project progressed too quickly; identified opportunities for improvement; and ensured shortcomings would not resurface on future projects.

David selected the precedence diagramming method (not to be confused with network diagramming in schedule calculations). He knew that this technique provides a thorough understanding and knowledge of how well project management processes are implemented for a specific project, focusing on people, quality, schedule, and cost. In addition, he recognized that risk management entails risk identification, risk analysis, risk control, and risk reporting. This requires that five simple steps be put in place.

Step 1: Acquire preliminary project background
Step 2: Conduct ranking/matrix construction
Step 3: Conduct in-depth review

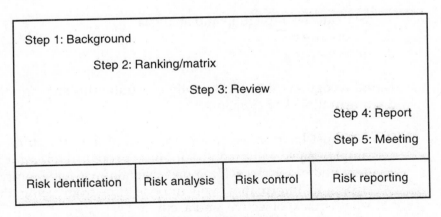

Fig 9.3 The five steps of risk management

Step 4: Prepare report/presentation
Step 5: Conduct meeting with senior management

These five steps correspond to risk management (see Figure 9.3).

Step 1: Acquire preliminary project background

To understand the key goals and issues for his project, David first collects several sources of information, including the following.

- Policies and procedures
- Data
- Project history files
- Project documentation
- Project manual
- Other literature

He collates the information and answers the questions who, what, when, where, why, and how. He thus can ask intelligent, meaningful questions during the sessions on the risk identification matrix and during follow-up reviews.

To gather the above information, David utilises three techniques:

1.   Statistical compilation and analysis
2.   Literature reviews
3.   Interviewing

David recognizes that successfully executing this step and Step 2 requires three key elements.

1.   He must have access to all resources of the project: for example, time, equipment, supplies, people, data/information, and office space. He knows that failure to have complete access to information will impede him from being thorough, quick, objective, and accurate.
2.   He needs three to five people to build the forthcoming ma-

trix (for Step 2). These people should be decision-makers and subject matter experts. They must be available for a maximum of two hours per session. Several sessions may be required.

3.   He also needs, most important of all, senior management to commit itself to the risk identification and analysis steps. He needs management to provide the time, people, and other resources so that the process provides a value-added service to the Yuggenheim Foundation.

Step 2: Conduct ranking/matrix construction

Two sub-steps are involved in Step 2: (a) to assemble the team, and (b) to rank goals and processes. Both these steps occur simultaneously.

Assemble the team
David knows that for this first sub-step, he must assemble a team of project experts. The team – facilitated by David – identifies and prioritizes the processes and goals of the project. Then, it ranks the processes and goals to provide the basis for determining the existence and importance of processes. It also ascertains whether the processes are efficiently and effectively attaining project goals.

David realizes that to perform an effective risk identification and analysis he requires a team of participants fulfilling four distinct roles. He also realizes that an instrumental tool in risk identification is the risk identification matrix – the result of extensive effort to identify, according to priority, the major goals and processes of the project and how effective the processes achieve those goals.

The four distinct roles are:

● Facilitator
● Subject matter experts
● Selected project team members
● Scribe

Facilitator
David is this person. He co-ordinates the entire identification process and, as the name implies, facilitates, not runs the session. He ensures the session is a meaningful event that enables expeditious risk identification.

Subject matter experts
David identifies the most knowledgeable people on the project. He determines who will attend the session(s) on the risk identification matrix and who to interview throughout the step.

Selected project team members
The people who attend the session to construct the project identification matrix are selected by David. He makes his selection based upon three criteria: experience, knowledge, and maturity. Often, subject matter experts are selected team members.

Scribe
This person takes the notes during the session on the risk identification matrix. David realizes he cannot be the scribe. Facilitating the session requires concentration; taking notes breaks that concentration. Therefore, he must assign someone else to take notes. That person should be a non-participant in the discussions.

With the right people available, David begins the sessions to build the identification matrix, playing an important facilitative role and making sure that:

1. He sets up the room before the session. All the equipment and furniture are located where he wants them. People are distracted if the facilitator at any meeting is still setting up equipment or moving furniture at the beginning. It takes away time which should be directed towards the goals and objectives of the meeting and breaks concentration.
2. He comes prepared. This point is allied to the first point. David should not only ensure that everything is in place for the session to run smoothly and effectively. He must also

ensure that the right supplies and equipment are to hand. Searching for or using makeshift materials is distractive.

3. He has nominated a scribe. The scribe is not a member of the team and is only employed to take notes. David and the team participants must concentrate on the goals and objectives of the meeting, which require their undivided attention. As facilitator, David will also want to be free to listen to the most important comments and insights of the participants, thereby allowing for more thorough risk identification.

4. He encourages everyone to speak at the session. A tendency exists for a few strong personalities to dominate, influencing the thought processes of other team members. The purpose of the session is to collect information about the project, not to provide a sounding board for the loudest or most talkative individual.

5. He seeks immediate agreement on definitions. People can easily lose themselves in semantics. Failure to clarify the meaning of words can result in a communications breakdown because different people operate on different 'wavelengths'.

6. He seeks agreement on perspective. As with semantics, it's important for everyone to understand each other. The best way to achieve understanding is for everyone to look at the project from the same perspective. This becomes absolutely critical when prioritizing the different processes and goals of a project. From what perspective is a goal more important than another? From a monetary perspective? From a schedule perspective? From a customer requirements perspective? And so on.

7. He remains noncommittal and objective. He avoids taking sides on any issue. Doing so means losing objectivity and may result in a loss of credibility. However, this does not mean not taking sides in facilitating the session itself. Sometimes he may have to overcome a deadlock or expedite the session.

8. He is confident everyone understands the purpose of the session and its procedures and rules. With this understand-

ing in place, participants can contribute and the session will proceed efficiently, effectively, and fairly.

9. He applies active listening skills. As a facilitator he must not only hear but listen. He must be attentive to comments and questions without filtering anything that agrees or disagrees with his thinking. Active listening is a quick way to encourage participation.

10. He distributes a handout with the agenda. Distributing anything during the session disrupts proceedings and directs people's attention away from the subject.

11. He gives breaks frequently. God gave us bladders of limited capacity and attention spans of short duration. To ensure alertness and full attention during the meeting, breaks should be frequent, say ten minutes every hour. Remember, the mind can absorb only what the kidneys can endure.

12. He schedules multiple sessions if the session is due to last several hours, say two hours or more. People prefer to attend short, more frequent sessions rather than a long one. However, keep multiple sessions to a minimum. Frequent sessions provide a greater opportunity to lose people, physically and emotionally.

Rank goals and processes

David is ready to draft the matrix with the team (see Figure 9.4). Notice that the matrix consists of:

- X-axis (goals)
- Y-axis (processes)
- Cells (degree of strength)

The *X-axis* contains the project goals, ranked from most to least important. The *Y-axis* contains the project processes also ranked, from the most important to least important. Each *cell* represents the relative degree of strength that measures exist to support achieving project goals.

Goal / Process	Schedule	Cost	Publicity	75% ratio
Planning	Strong	Moderate	Strong	Weak
Leading	Weak	Moderate	Weak	Weak
Organizing	Strong	Strong	Weak	Strong
Closure	Weak	Weak	Weak	Weak
Controlling	Weak	Moderate	Strong	Moderate
Assessment	Strong	Moderate	Weak	Weak
Definition	Weak	Weak	Moderate	Strong

Fig 9.4   Final project matrix (example)

Step 3: Conduct in-depth review

Identifying the goals (X-axis) for each process (Y-axis) can come from several sources. Although a project manager may list one goal, having several goals is not uncommon. A goal(s) is often a broad statement reflecting what the project will achieve. It may be vague ('customer satisfaction') or specific ('produce a system with a maximum response time of five seconds').

David and the risk identification and analysis team may not have a clear idea of the goal(s) of the project. For further clarification, he might ask them to review project documentation, such as the statement of work, work breakdown structure, policy statements, memorandums, and practices. They may also interview project leadership and clients to understand wants and needs and identify any concerns regarding goals.

Once the team determines the goal(s), the next task is to rank the goals according to importance. An objective way to accomplish this is through a forced ranking technique. The latter technique requires the team to determine which goal is more important *vis-à-vis* another (see Figure 9.5).

Throughout the ranking activity, David is the individual who asks which goal is more important *vis-à-vis* another.

Forced ranking technique
Each session participant has one vote and can split it. The number of votes for each goal is tallied vertically and horizontally and then added together. For example, Cost has a total score of 5 horizontally and a vertical score of 4. The sum of the two numbers equals 9.

David repeats this exercise for all the goals listed. The goal with the highest number is the most important while the goal with the smallest number is the least important. Later, David reorders the goals to reflect this priority.

The session participants now identify the seven major processes which exist for the project. (These seven can be exploded into sub-processes, if necessary, but will not occur for this case study.) The seven processes are:

	Publicity	Schedule	Cost	75% ratio
Publicity		1	2	3
Schedule	4		3	3
Cost	3	**2**		4
75% ratio	2	2	1	
. . .				
. . .				
. . .				
	6	6	4	0

0 + 6 = 6   4 + 6 = 10   5 + 4 = 9   5 + 0 = 5

Fig 9.5   Ranking of RAW project goals

Note: Publicity – provides high publicity for the project
Schedule – complete the project on schedule
Cost – keep costs within budget
75% ratio – retain a 75% exotic animals ratio

1. Leading: influencing people to achieve goals and objectives of the project.
2. Assessment: determining the environment in which a project must occur.
3. Definition: deciding in advance the goals of the project.
4. Planning: determining what steps to execute, assigning who will perform those tasks, and verifying when they must start and stop.
5. Organizing: orchestrating resources cost-effectively to execute project plans.
6. Controlling: assessing how well the project manager uses plans and organization to meet project goals and objectives.
7. Closure: completing the project efficiently and effectively.

Once the identification reveals the processes, the participants must rank the processes according to importance. The same forced ranking technique used for goal prioritization is used. This technique requires participants to determine which process is more important *vis-à-vis* another. Throughout the ranking activity, the facilitator, David, is the only individual who asks which process is more important than another.

After identifying and prioritizing goals and processes, David and his team calculate the results.

Each session participant has one vote and can split it. The number of votes for each process is tallied vertically and horizontally and then added together. For example, Organizing has a total score of 12 horizontally and a vertical score of 5. The sum of the two numbers equals 17. David repeats this exercise for all the processes listed. The process with the highest number is the most important while the process with the smallest value is the least important. Later, David reorders to reflect this priority. An example of ranking processes is shown in Figure 9.6.

It is not necessary that participants be present during any calculations. The mathematical calculation, which is mainly addition and multiplication, is labour intensive and will only bore participants. David considers rescheduling the meeting to review the results of the calculations.

Fig 9.6 Ranking of RAW project processes

	Identification	Leading	Definition	Planning	Organizing	Controlling	Closure
Identification	Identification 0 + 12 = 12						
Leading	3 / 2	Leading 2 + 15.5 = 17.5					
Definition	2 / 3	5 / 0	Definition 3 + 5.5 = 8.5				
Planning	1 / 4	2.5 / 2.5	2.5 / 2.5	Planning 9 + 11 = 20			
Organizing	2 / 3	1 / 4	1 / 4	4 / 1	Organizing 12 + 5 = 17		
Controlling	4 / 1	5 / 0	0 / 5	3 / 2	5 / 0	Controlling 8 + 5 = 13	
Closure	0 / 5	2 / 3	2 / 3	4 / 1	0 / 5	5 / 0	Closure 17 + 0 = 17
	12	15.5	5.5	11	5	5	0

133

Determining quadrants

The next action for David is to group the cells into quadrants to prioritize the former. See Figure 9.7 for a matrix showing four quadrants as 1, 2 and 3, and 4. The first quadrant is the most important group of cells, the second and third quadrants are the next most important, and the fourth quadrant is the least important. Determining these quadrants is based upon the mathematical calculation for each cell.

On the X-axis, David organizes the goals in descending priority using earlier calculations (refer to Figure 9.5). He ensures that the calculated number for that goal appears underneath the narrative description. For example, the Schedule goal has a value of 10 which appears under its heading. David then repeats that step for the processes on the Y-axis. Again, he ensures that the calculated value for that process appears underneath the narrative description. For example, organizing has a value of 17 which appears under Organizing (refer to Figure 9.6)

Next, David calculates the value for each cell. This is determined by multiplying the value of a specific goal times the value of a specific process. The product of the two represents the value for that cell. For example, Organizing has a value of 17 and Schedule has a value of 10. Its cell value is therefore 170. David repeats this calculation for all the cells in the matrix.

After completing the calculations, he determines the quadrants. This is arrived at by grouping the values in descending order and then identifying the top 25 per cent numbers (1st quadrant), the next 25 per cent (2nd quadrant), the next 25 per cent (third quadrant), and the bottom 25 per cent (4th quadrant). If a tie results, David arbitrarily decides whether that cell should be a higher or lower quadrant, preferably the former. One way is to toss a coin or conduct another round of voting to resolve a tie.

For each example in Figure 9.7 there are four goals and seven processes: $4 \times 7 = 28$ cells. These cells are arranged in descending priority order horizontally and vertically. Thus, 25 per cent of the 28 cells (25 per cent $\times$ 28) equals 7 cells per quadrant. The first quadrant, however, contains eight items since a tie (a value

Process \ Goal	Schedule (10)	Cost (9)	Publicity (6)	75% ratio (5)
Planning (20)	200	180 **1**	120	100 **2,3**
Leading (17.5)	175	157.5	105	87.5
Organizing (17)	**170**	153	102	85
Closure (17)	170	153	102	85
Controlling (13)	130	117 **2,3**	78	65 **4**
Assessment (12)	120	108	72	60
Definition (8.5)	85	76.5	51	42.5

Fig 9.7 Matrix showing quadrants

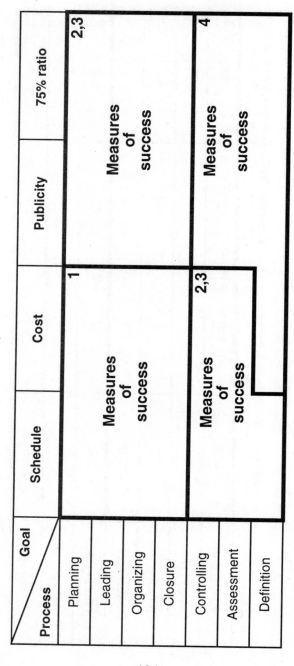

Fig 9.8 How measures of success relate to matrix

136

of 153) exists between Organizing and Closure. The second and third quadrants represent 13 cells, or approximately 50 per cent; and the fourth quadrant represent 7 cells, or 25 per cent.

David is now ready to evaluate how well the controls, or measures of success, are in place to achieve project goals (see Figure 9.8). Evaluation is achieved by identifying the measures of success for each cell. In Figures 9.10 to 9.16 the measures of success for each process are shown. These measures apply to any goal on a project. (An index for each process and its related measures of success is shown in Figure 9.9.)

Process	Measures of success figure number
Planning	9.10
Leading	9.11
Organizing	9.12
Closure	9.13
Controlling	9.14
Assessment	9.15
Definition	9.16

Fig 9.9   Index of process *vis-à-vis* measure of success by figure number

---

Does a work breakdown structure exist?

Are reliable time and cost estimates available?

Has risk control been conducted?

Have resources been allocated?

Does a reliable schedule exist?

Fig 9.10   Measures of success – Planning

Does a vision exist?

Is there a communications plan?

Are incentives being used to motivate project participants?

Is the project proceeding according to plan?

Does the environment facilitate performance?

Are techniques for effective team-building being used?

Fig 9.11   Measures of success – Leading

Is project management software selected?

Is there an effective team organization?

Are project procedures available?

Are project history files available?

Are useful forms available?

Are the right reports being produced?

Is a project library available?

Are memos prepared when appropriate?

Is a newsletter published?

Does a project office exist?

Are project manuals published?

Fig 9.12   Measures of success – Organizing

Are statistics being compiled?

Is a lessons learned document being produced?

Will there be a post-implementation review?

Are winding-down activities occurring?

Fig 9.13   Measures of success – Closure

Is status collection being performed?

Is status assessment being conducted?

Are the appropriate meetings being held?

Are change control activities occurring?

Is replanning occurring?

Are corrective actions being taken?

Fig 9.14   Measures of success – Controlling

Has an assessment of the company's history of project management been done?

Has an assessment of the project's environment been done?

Are all the key players identified?

Are the project management practices the company does well identified?

Are the policies, procedures, practices, etc. affecting project management identified?

Fig 9.15   Measures of success – Assessment

Are there goals and objectives for the project?

Is there a Statement of Work?

Has a project announcement been published?

Have the roles and responsibilities for project participants been documented? Have they been communicated to participants? Have they been agreed to?

Has the project launch meeting been held?

Is the Statement of Work signed off?

Fig 9.16   Measures of success – Definition

Using these measures of success, David determines whether their application for an applicable cell are strong, moderate, or weak. He determines that through the cell evaluation scheme in Figure 9.17. This procedure applies to all cells.

For each measure of success applicable to a cell, David determines to what degree the measure has been applied on a project. The degree is strong, moderate, or weak, each worth 3, 2, and 1 points, respectively. The entire column for strong is added, then moderate, and finally weak. The three results are added together and divided by the total possible score for all the items in that cell (which is 3 points times all the number of measures for that cell), resulting in a percentage. This percentage reflects the combined degree that the measures of success for a process have been applied to achieve a particular goal of a project.

David uses the scale (in Figure 9.18) to evaluate the combined degree.

David's judgement relies upon his experience and knowledge. Of course, the more assessors like David that participate in the judgement the greater the objectivity of the results. He

Measures of success / Evaluation	Strong (3)	Moderate (2)	Weak (1)
Has an assessment of the company's history of project management been done?	X		
Has an assessment of the project's environment been done?		X	
Are all the key players identified?			X
Are the project management practices the company does well identified?		X	
Are the policies, procedures, practices, etc. affecting project management identified?		X	
Total:	3	6	1

Grand total = Strong [3 × 1] + Moderate [2 × 3] + Weak [1 × 1] = 10
Maximum score = Strong [3 × 5 line items] = 15
This project's evaluation = 10/15 = 66% which falls into the moderate rating (see Figure 9.18)

Fig 9.17   Cell evaluation scheme assessment

can obtain the necessary information to make such judgements from numerous sources. For example, he can interview project participants, review project documentation, witness project activities, and compile and analyse data.

After completing all the calculations, David produces a matrix (see Figure 9.19).

100–75%	Strong
74–25%	Moderate
24–0%	Weak

Fig 9.18   Cell evaluation

Put in final form

David can prepare the final matrix (as in Figure 9.19), in one of several ways. He can use graphs, spreadsheet, word processing software, or some other combination. The software medium depends on his own preferences. Regardless of medium, the matrix should be:

- Clean
- Clear
- Complete
- Concise
- Consistent

Step 4: Prepare report/presentation

After preparing the final matrix, David is now ready to present the results. His two principal audiences are the team members who participated in constructing the matrix and senior management. The reason for presenting to the team members is to verify the accuracy and contents of the final matrix. The reason for presenting to senior management is to present the significant findings to help them make important decisions about the project.

David presents the results either orally or in written form.

Goal Process	Schedule	Cost	Publicity	75% ratio
Planning	Strong	Moderate	Strong	Weak
Leading	Weak	Moderate	Weak	Weak
Organizing	Strong	Strong	Weak	Strong
Closure	Weak	Weak	Weak	Weak
Controlling	Weak	Moderate	Strong	Moderate
Assessment	Strong	Moderate	Weak	Weak
Definition	Weak	Weak	Moderate	Strong

Fig 9.19 RAW project final report matrix

144

Structure of written report

The written report should have the following structure:

- Cover page
- Background
- Scope
- Findings
- Recommendations

The cover page presents the report title, date, recipients, and the name of the assessor(s) – in this case David Michaels. The background gives the history leading to the risk identification, such as the name of the requester, start date, and initiating factors. The scope describes what was covered and omitted in the identification and analysis, the level of detail, and the goals and objectives. The findings describe those measures of success needing improvement and their impact on the project. The recommendations present ways to improve the measures of success.

In preparing his written report, David will:

- Stress in the scope of the report that the matrix follows a qualitative, not quantitative, approach. Although it involves some calculations, the risk identification and analysis does not entail complex calculations dealing with probabilities and regression analysis. It is a straightforward method that provides management and project managers with a quick and efficient way to assess project performance without impacting operations.
- Write clearly and concisely. Wordiness not only confuses the reader but also bores them. David wants the reader to understand his message immediately and to know what needs improvement.
- Avoid spelling errors. Nothing kills the credibility of a report more quickly than spelling errors. Most word processing packages have spell checkers and not using them indicates bad judgement. This will reflect badly on the author of the report and call into question, true or not, that judgement contained in the report.

- Attach and reference the matrix. David ensures that the matrix accompanies the report and references it throughout the document. It doesn't make much sense to prepare a matrix that no one sees while reading the report.
- Keep the report within three to five A4 pages. Lengthy reports often go unread. David also balances the sub-sections of the report, using a rule of thumb (see Figure 9.20).

Cover page	5%
Background	5%
Scope	5%
Findings	70%
Recommendations	15%
Total	100%

Fig 9.20   Rule of thumb for reports

- Ensure that the distribution list is accurate and complete. David also ensures that everyone having an interest in the results of the risk identification and analysis receives a copy. By including all the appropriate participants, they have ownership of the entire process and do not feel 'shut out'. Proper distribution eliminates the opportunity for individuals to cry 'foul'.

Finally, and allied to the previous point, David encourages review of the draft in advance of publication. He ensures that the individuals affected by the results have a chance to review it. He knows that this action lessens the opportunity for people to take offence and oppose the findings. Figure 9.21 presents a sample written report.

```
                Yuggenheim Foundation
                     RAW Project
                Risk Management Report

     20 December 19XX

     To:   Craig Yuggenheim
     cc:   Nicole Boyer
           Richard Cooper
           Tonia Elizabeth
           Bill Holmes
           Melissa Nicole

     Assessor:  David Michaels
```

Background

   The Yuggenheim Foundation wants to add a wild
animal 'park', called RAW, *R*oaming *A*nimals of
the *W*ilderness, to the new zoo that was built
after the Zoo Dismantling Project was completed
(see Figure 9.1). Craig Yuggenheim, the CEO,
wants David Michaels to manage the RAW project.
The Foundation expects to generate approximately
$150 million a year in net revenue from the
park. By law, however, the Foundation cannot use
any of the resources or revenue of the adjacent
zoo. Otherwise, tax problems arise and the
Yuggenheim Foundation may lose its tax-exempt
status.

Scope

   Before starting any construction, Mr Yuggenheim
wants to see a risk management plan consisting
of risk identification, risk analysis, risk
control, and risk reporting.

Fig 9.21   Improvements for effective team-building

Craig Yuggenheim noted four goals for the project:

- Provide high publicity for the project
- Complete the project on schedule
- Keep construction costs within budget
- Retain a 75 per cent exotic animals ratio

Findings
In David's report there are several areas (designated as weak) for improvement (see Figure 9.9).

The Leading process and the Schedule goal, in the first and highest priority quadrant, show a weak relationship for several measures of success. Techniques for effective team-building are not being used. The staff each has their own agenda. The impact is that shared deliverables will not be accomplished unless there is alignment and co-operation of all teams necessary to make the RAW a reality.

Recommendations
Improvements for effective team-building might include:

- Jointly train the general contractor and the Yuggenheim staff in Yuggenheim team-building practices and conduct
- Follow-up on practices after completion of training
- Expedite long lead times for critical equipment
- Work directly with supplier, not middleman

Fig 9.21   concluded

Oral presentation

The structure of David's presentation follows the format of the written report. It has a cover sheet and the same sections. The contents of the session, like the written report, should be clear, concise, accurate, and comprehensive.[2]

When giving the oral presentation, David will:

- Arrive on time. Failure to arrive on time reflects, albeit perhaps not correctly, that he does not think the session is very important.
- Use slides that are clear and understandable. He won't try to pack everything on a slide; he will show only what is necessary to prove a point. He will also ensure that everyone can read the slides, not just the people sitting in the front row.
- Avoid rushing into details. His presentation is structured, giving an overview and background and information in the beginning and then providing the details. This structure deters listeners from turning away during the session.
- Distribute copies after the presentation. Distributing them during the presentation only distracts from remarks. It's permissible to give out copies of the report prior to the presentation but David recognizes that not everyone will read it. Those listeners who do will have a decided advantage over those who do not, which can make receptivity to findings and recommendations difficult.
- Allow time for questions and answers. With a questions and answers session, people have an opportunity to clarify vague notions and misunderstandings affecting their receptivity towards the report's findings and recommendations.
- Notify the right people. These being the managers and selected individuals who participated in the sessions to construct the matrix. Ensuring that they all attend the presentation assures a greater likelihood of receptivity and feedback on findings and recommendations.
- Remain flexible, allow for changes. David recognizes the possibility that during the final presentation he may – acci-

dentally or deliberately – omit important information. He may not have the opportunity to realize or appreciate the importance of this omission until later.

- Stress the confidentiality of findings. Some information will inevitably embarrass some people. It's important to understand that the release of the identification and analysis

```
                Yuggenheim Foundation
                    RAW Project
                Risk Management Report

    20 December 19XX

    To:  Craig Yuggenheim
    cc:  Nicole Boyer
         Richard Cooper
         Tonia Elizabeth
         Bill Holmes
         Melissa Nicole

    Assessor:  David Michaels
```

Fig 9.22a   (Cover page – 5 per cent)

```
                    Background


    • Yuggenheim Foundation

        -  Annex RAW to new zoo

        -  Net revenue US$150 million per year
```

Fig 9.22b   (Background – 5 per cent)

results is the decision of the client, not David. (For a view of David's oral presentation, see Figures 9.22a–9.22e.)

```
                        Scope

                     Four goals


    ●  Provide high publicity for the project

    ●  Complete the project on schedule

    ●  Keep construction costs within budget

    ●  Retain a 75 per cent exotic animals ratio
```

Fig 9.22c   (Scope – 5 per cent)

```
                      Findings

                 Areas for Improvements


    ●  Leading vs. Schedule

       –  Techniques for effective      Deliverables
          team-building                 not met

       –  Project may not proceed       Delay opening
          as planned                    by 6 months
```

Fig 9.22d   (Findings – 70 per cent)

```
                    Recommendations


  ●  Leading vs. Schedule

       -  Techniques for effective      Jointly train
          team-building                  general con-
                                         tractor and
                                         Yuggenheim
                                         staff

                                         Follow up
                                         after training
                                         is complete

       -  Project may not proceed       Expedite long
          as planned                     lead times for
                                         critical
                                         equipment

                                         Work directly
                                         with supplier,
                                         not middleman
```

Fig 9.22e   (Recommendations – 15 per cent)

Step 5: Conduct meeting with senior management

David Michaels uses the final report matrix (see Figure 9.19) to answer these two simple questions:

- What are the current risks to the RAW project?
- Where are the vulnerabilities that will hinder the attainment of project goals?

He now knows the answers to these two questions without having to significantly disrupt his life or obtain a PhD in mathematics. The approach he uses is 'KISS', an acronym for *Keep It Super Simple*. His presentation is easy to follow, accurate, and meaningful to everyone.

Meaningful insights

When meeting with senior management, David:

- Will highlight the areas needing improvement but will not ignore the positives. He will also avoid the temptation to be a zealot or an auditor with a taste for blood. His presentation of the matrix is a meaningful service to senior management.
- Will not finger-point. True, some findings will inevitably pinpoint some people. However, the issue is not with the person but with the process and with its implementation. The report criticizes ideas or processes, not people. Only management and the project manager have the right to finger-point, if they elect to do so. Otherwise, project managers will become involved in the internal politics of their projects which can only hurt their credibility.
- Will, with reference to the preceding insight, concentrate on the identification and analysis steps. He will identify what's strong, moderate, or weak about the processes. Such concentration helps project managers to remain objective and protects their credibility.
- Will produce composite results. Directing attention to the process, more often than not, involves more than one person. By doing so, project managers avoid finger-pointing. In addition, they avoid the temptation to quibble over details rather than discuss broader, more important issues.
- Will keep all findings confidential. This practice avoids embarrassing people and engenders a sense of trust and mutual respect. Breach confidentiality and project managers wreck their credibility, too.
- Will emphasize that the results do not guarantee project success. Too many variables exist for project managers to

predict project results. Personality and management styles are examples of individuals' variables that influence the outcome of any project. The best that project managers under any circumstance can do is suggest improvements that will only increase the likelihood of future project success.

- Will advise that the basis for results are 'as is' conditions of the project, not prescriptive. The results highlight areas for improvement now so that project performance in the future will have a greater likelihood of improvement. The project manager's recommendations, however, should not come across as 'this is what you should have done or should do'. Ultimately, David will leave the decision to senior management to accept or reject his recommendations.

Part IV
The Future of Risk Management

10 High Risk in the New Millennium

It's quite apparent that the importance of project risk will continue to grow. Practically every industry is going through great transition, from telecommunications and information systems to retail and banking services. Projects now involve greater sums of money; must deliver products of high quality, at a lower cost and faster pace than was the case 50, even 25, years ago. All this to be accomplished and at the same time satisfy customers' precise needs. 'Cheaper, better, and faster' is the phrase that best describes projects for the next millennium.

Macro-trends

There are twelve 'macro-trends' which increase the risks that projects must face. Their effect on projects makes it difficult to deliver on time, and within budget, and maintain the highest level of quality. These macro-trends are already greatly impacting projects, highlighting the importance of risk management to an unprecedented level. These macro-trends are:

1. Building highly complex products
2. Relying on multiple data sources
3. Taking a cross-functional approach
4. Aligning project management with strategic planning
5. Accelerating product lead time, from concept to market
6. Customizing the product to satisfy customer requirements
7. Internationalizing the market place
8. Contracting and outsourcing services
9. Encouraging greater partnership and ownership by participants
10. Decentralizing operations
11. Applying greater technical expertise
12. Relying on more sophisticated tools

Building highly complex products

Projects in today's world are unparalleled in complexity. This does not imply that projects in earlier times were any easier. As technology evolves, however, so does the complexity behind each generation of a product. In other words, each technological solution generates new complications, adding a level of difficulty not previously experienced. For example, many subjects once considered only theoretical possibilities are today realities: fibre optics, lasers, world wide web, electronic data interchange, robotics, wireless computing, image processing, neural nets, genetic mapping, miniaturization, digital high-definition television, virtual reality, client/server computing, cellular telephones – the list seems endless.

These products and many others present considerable complexity, largely technical in nature. Such complexity inevitably brings with it several risks, making it difficult to complete a project on time, within budget, and of high quality.

Technical failure is a risk that can occur in building highly complex products. Regardless of the money, time, or resources available to a project, if the product doesn't work the project is suspended or halts altogether. Inability to resolve technical complexities quickly is another risk. With complexity comes greater opportunities for problems to arise: unless they are surmounted quickly, either in the form of a 'quick patch' or by tracing their true source, the schedule will inevitably slip and costs will in-crease.

Relying on multiple data sources

In earlier days, project participants could access data and infor-mation by using books or a mainframe computer or both. To-day, they can access a wide array of data and information, thanks to advances in micro-size and mid-size computing, distributed systems, and decentralized information systems (IS). In addi-tion, the IS environment has become more open: no longer is it constrained by specific hardware and software standards. Ac-cess to data, located anywhere in the world, is possible with technologies like the world wide web.

Reliance on multiple data sources raises issues that, up to now, were rarely addressed by project managers: access rights to data; security of hardware, software, and data; and reliability, integrity, and relevance of data.

These issues pose certain risks to projects. First, using inaccu-rate or poor data to make decisions which, in turn, results in inaccurate or poor decisions. Decisions based on such data can send a project down the wrong path. Second, the introduction of viruses. Removing viruses takes time and money, thereby affecting schedule and budget performance.

Taking a cross-functional approach

With the rise and application of continuous quality improve-ment (CQI) and business process re-engineering (BPR), project participants recognize that their projects no longer function in isolation. A project is a system which, in turn, is part of a much larger system. Project team members approach their task with an enterprise-wide, or gestalt view, of their projects. They are more inclined to identify how macro- and micro-processes in-terrelate and affect not only their own project's progress but also that of others.

Such interdependency helps build smoother working rela-tionships and better project performance. But potential risks arise. First, a gestalt view can lead to complexity in planning. Simplicity in approach fades into the background along with shorter planning sessions, and schedule completion dates begin to slip. Second, a cross-functional viewpoint can hinder the team's ability to respond quickly to changing situations. Project participants find they must over-analyse situations to unravel complexities, called analysis paralysis (see Chapter 2), resulting in schedule delays.

Aligning project management with strategic planning

In the past, many companies treated project management and strategic planning as two separate techniques. Very little tracking occurred against the value of the project and a company's strategic plan. In large institutions, a project often went on for years despite radically altered strategic plans.

Today, the linkage between project management and strategic planning exists in many organizations. Project goals and objectives are aligned with those of the company, thanks to project managers understanding the 'big picture' and also to senior management recognizing well-managed projects as a means to gain strategic advantage in the market-place.

While this linkage is positive, a risk can arise. Closely linking project management with a strategic plan can inhibit the ability or the desire to innovate. The reason is that anything construed as being not within the strategic plan can be ignored. Such a view halts projects or discounts ideas that, at the time, appear irrelevant in the short run but may well prove beneficial to the company game plan in the long run.

Accelerating product lead time, from concept to market

Getting a high-quality product to market at a competitive price is no longer enough. The rise of the global economy is increasing the number of competitors offering products of high quality at a reasonable price; late delivery can mean lost customers. Accelerating the time to complete a project may be critical to a company's survival. Time-based project management, therefore, is as important as quality-based project management when the market has many able competitors and becomes so dynamic that any delay turns a project into an anachronism.

This acceleration in the market-place poses risks to projects. First, it encourages project participants to 'cut corners,' thereby increasing the potential for sacrificing quality; re-work arises that may contribute to schedule slippage and higher labour costs. Second, there is a tendency to create waste in labour, materials, supplies and so on, in order to meet market deadlines. The old adage 'haste makes waste' applies: rushing to complete a project may meet the schedule but may also damage reputation and increase support costs.

Customizing the product to satisfy customer requirements

The customer has become king according to quality and productivity research theory: activity-based costing (ABC), BPR, component-based manufacturing, and TQM are examples.

In such an atmosphere, user-centred project management becomes highly important and the engine for planning, organizing, controlling, and leading projects from the perspective of the user.

However, when the customer is king a new risk can arise – the customer's indecisiveness or lack of co-operation. Where this risk occurs it causes considerable schedule delays and substantial re-work.

Internationalizing the market-place

The market-place is no longer regional or national – it's international. With internationalization comes more competition from more companies. The complexity of internationalization manifests itself when projects call on global resources to build their products. Such interdependency increases the complexity of a project, internal and external. For example, a project requires hardware components for computing equipment from both Japan and the United States; failure to receive components from Japan results in schedule slippage. This escalates project costs as, too, does the search for an alternative supplier. The project manager has minimal control in such a situation.

Hence, internationalization poses several risks to projects. A project may be unable to plan thoroughly because market conditions change rapidly, mainly due to external economic and political forces. For example, should the Chinese reduce export of a mineral used in the manufacture of a new aircraft in another country, the project will possibly be delayed or may even have to be cancelled. It is often the case that unpredictability in the market-place leads to unrealistic project planning because too many extraneous factors exist to devise anything realistic.

Contracting and outsourcing services

In an effort to lower costs, many companies contract or outsource services. This enables them to do what they do best and reduce operating costs. Indeed, it is not uncommon today for companies to outsource 'administrative' functions to a third party or external supplier. For example, many computing firms contract out programming services.

Contracting and outsourcing services in this way raises issues such as reliability and performance, as well as dependency on external suppliers. From a project management perspective, there are several risks to assess. First, that of adequate oversight of work, to avoid poor quality and re-work costs. Second, dependency on an external supplier, which could negatively affect schedule and budget performance.

Encouraging greater partnership and ownership by participants

Thanks largely to the behavioural management movement, more decision-making processes are developing, or flowing down, to the people who do the work. This trend has affected the management of projects where sharing decision-making and delegating tasks have become commonplace on medium-size and large projects.

Undoubtedly, there are many benefits in adopting this approach, chiefly encouragement of pride and ownership of output. However, two risks are present. First, the increase in time and effort required to make a decision and reach a consensus – which, until attained, creates schedule delays. Second, empowerment makes it difficult for people to move in the same direction. Unless unity is achieved, again, schedule delays will result.

Decentralizing operations

Thanks also in large part to the behavioural management movement, companies are increasingly operating in a more unstructured manner. This trend improves flexibility and encourages responsibility for performance. Decentralization affects project performance, too. Rigid structures and other administrative hurdles (for example, receiving approval before taking action) are fading, albeit gradually in some areas. New concepts – virtual corporations, network-based organizations, self-managed work teams – are becoming reality in the project arena, replacing command and control management styles.

There are also risks inherent in decentralizing operations. First, the difficulty in getting people to co-ordinate with one another; and, second, the difficulty in gaining consensus over important issues. Both difficulties cause schedule delays.

Applying greater technical expertise

Despite the overwhelming cry for generalists, the demand continues to grow for specialists. The reason is that products, evolving to an unprecedented level of complexity, require people with an in-depth knowledge and skill of a particular subject. Knowledge workers with a narrow expertise must define, design, and develop sophisticated parts of a product.

This trend towards greater specialization poses risks to projects. First, poor communications can occur resulting from jargon and the esoteric nature of specializations, thereby causing schedule delays and poor workmanship. Second, inadequate co-ordination due to specialists working independently which, again, can result in schedule delays, poor workmanship, and high frustration. Third, specialists become obsolete, thereby causing morale to drop and the quality of workmanship to decline.

Relying on more sophisticated tools

Tool utilization has become a prominent ingredient in enhancing productivity in organizations in general and projects in particular. In today's world, tools require access to information (such as through the world wide web) and require compatibility (such as between hardware and software).

MACRO-TREND	RISK	POSSIBLE CONTINGENCY PLAN
1. Building highly complex products	Technical failure	• Perform feasibility study prior to project • Conduct benchmark of similar projects
	Inability to resolve technical complexities quickly	• Hire additional expertise • Produce products in versions • Use 'reusable' tested products
2. Relying on multiple databases	Inaccurate or poor data to make decisions	• Cross-check existing data with other sources • Upgrade or purge data periodically
	Introduction of viruses	• Use virus checkers • Restrict access to microcomputers
3. Tracking a cross-functional approach	Complexity in planning	• Produce products in versions • Build models or prototypes first
	Inability to respond quickly to changing conditions	• Set deadlines for decisions • Restrict number of participants in the

Fig 10.1 Some contingency plans for managing risks associated with macro-trends

MACRO-TREND	RISK	POSSIBLE CONTINGENCY PLAN
4. Aligning project management with strategic planning	Inhibit ability or desire to innovate	• Encourage 'threat-free' environment • Reward innovative, value-added ideas
5. Accelerating product lead time, from concept to market	Project participants cut corners	• Require cross-check of work • Produce products in versions
	Tendency to create waste	• Review project processes • Require checkpoint reviews throughout life cycle
6. Customizing the product to satisfy customer requirements	Indecisiveness or unco-operativeness by customer	• Require customer approval before proceeding • Encourage customer participation throughout the project life cycle
7. Internationalizing the market-place	Unable to plan thoroughly	• Produce products in versions • Benchmark projects of a similar nature
	Unrealistic planning	• Produce products in versions • Use reliable estimating techniques

Fig 10.1 continued

MACRO-TREND	RISK	POSSIBLE CONTINGENCY PLAN
8. Contracting and outsourcing services	Inadequate oversight of work	• Periodically visit third-party sites • Require third parties to participate in status sessions
	Dependency on external supplier	• Have penalty payment for failure to deliver • Have list of alternative suppliers
9. Encourage greater partnership and ownership by participants	Excessive time and effort to make a decision	• Set deadlines for decisions • Restrict participation in the decision-making process
	Difficulty in getting people to move in the same direction	• Communicate plans • Hold frequent information sessions about the project

Fig 10.1 continued

MACRO-TREND	RISK	POSSIBLE CONTINGENCY PLAN
10. Decentralizing operations	Difficulty in getting people to co-ordinate with one another	• Hold frequent meetings • Publish project plans
	Difficulty in gaining consensus over important issues	• Hold frequent information-sharing sessions • Establish deadlines to resolve issues
11. Applying greater technical expertise	Poor communications	• Hold frequent information-sharing sessions • Publish project documentation
	Inadequate co-ordination	• Publish project plans • Hold frequent meetings
12. Relying on more sophisticated tools	Working with antiquated tools	• Negotiate with vendors to receive upgrades
	Use of incompatible tools	• Establish standards for tools • Purchase tools from same vendor

Fig 10.1   concluded

Two risks arise due to this reliance on sophisticated tools. First, project members may soon find they are working with antiquated tools, overtaken by superior technology thereby affecting the quality of workmanship and the level of morale. Second, frustration can arise if they continue to use incompatible tools, thereby lowering productivity and causing schedule delays.

Risky reality

Managing projects in today's environment is a challenging undertaking; there are many obstacles to success. Project managers can't fight these macro-trends but they can prepare themselves to manage the resulting impacts to their projects. Figure 10.1 provides possible contingency plans for dealing with some of the project risks caused by these macro-trends. The best approach, of course, is to use risk management – identification, analysis, control, and reporting – to bring a project in on time, within budget, and of the highest workmanship.

Appendices

Appendix A
A Five-step Process for Conducting Risk Identification and Analysis

The approach used in the case study in Part III works best for project managers if they follow the steps in this appendix. Throughout the case study, David Michaels sought to be objective, thorough, and empathetic. He continually recognized that he was providing a service that offers value-added findings and recommendations and not indicting project participants. He realized his credibility and reputation were always at stake. His step-by-step procedure for conducting risk identification and analysis is the subject of this appendix (see Figure A1.1).

Step 1: Acquire preliminary project background

Step 2: Conduct session(s) on the project assessment matrix

Step 3: Conduct in-depth review

Step 4: Prepare report

Step 5: Conduct meeting with senior management

Fig A1.1   Summary of five steps

171

Step 1: Acquire preliminary project background

A. Determine project goals and objectives. Possible sources of information include:

- Interviews
- Memorandums
- Policy statements
- Statement of work

B. Identify the major participants. Possible sources of information include:

- Memorandums
- Organization charts
- Project charters
- Responsibility matrices
- Statement of work
- Word of mouth

C. Acquire a description of the product or service for delivery. Possible sources of information include:

- Design documentation
- Interviews
- Product literature
- Statement of work
- Work breakdown structure

D. Review project plans. Possible sources of information include:

- Disaster/recovery plan
- Implementation plan
- Interviews
- Project history files
- Project manual
- Resource histograms

- Schedules
- Statement of work
- Work breakdown structure

E. Perform data compilation and analysis. Possible sources of information include:

- Cost estimates
- Metrics on quality
- Payback policies
- Time estimates
- Trends

F. Determine who, by name, to invite to the session(s) to build the risk identification matrix.

G. For the risk identification matrix session, determine who will perform the following roles:

- Facilitator
- Other team members
- Scribe
- Subject matter experts

H. To ensure success for the risk identification session, check for the following:

- Three to five people available for session
- Access to resources
- Adequate availability of time, equipment, and supplies
- Adequate conference room size
- Commitment from senior management

Step 2: Conduct session(s) on the project identification matrix

A. Assemble the team for the session.

B. Do the following items regarding the risk identification matrix session:

- Agree on definitions
- Agree on perspective
- Apply active listening skills
- Break frequently
- Come prepared
- Distribute handout with the agenda
- Encourage everyone to speak
- Ensure that the scribe is notified ahead of time and is not a team member
- Ensure everyone understands the objectives and processes
- Remain noncommittal/objective
- Set up room prior to the session
- Use multiple sessions but keep to a minimum

C. Determine the goals of the project. Possible sources of information might include:

- Discussions among members of the identification and analysis team
- Interviews
- Memorandums
- Policy statements
- Statement of work
- Work breakdown structure

D. Obtain consensus over what perspective to take when determining the priority of goals and processes, taking the perspective from one of these items:

- Budget
- Competition
- Personnel
- Quality
- Schedule

E. Obtain consensus over all terms that may have multiple interpretations.

- Document definitions of terms
- Document roles and responsibilities

F. Determine priority of the goals using the forced choice technique.

1. Copy the step form provided at the end of this appendix.
2. Ask all team members to vote on which goal is more important. (It is permissible for a team member to split their vote in half.)
3. Calculate the value for each goal by first adding the vertical scores in the applicable column for a goal and then adding the horizontal scores in the appropriate row for the same goal.
4. Identify the importance of a goal according to descending value. The higher the score the more valuable a goal is from the perspective of the team members.
5. Record the new prioritization of goals on the X-axis of a blank matrix form provided at the end of this appendix. (Record the value of the goals in brackets or parentheses.)

G. Determine priority of project processes using the forced choice technique.

1. Copy the step form provided at the end of this appendix.
2. Ask all team members to vote on which process is more important. (It is permissible for a team member to split their vote in half.)
3. Calculate the value for each process by first adding the

vertical scores in the applicable column for a process and then adding the horizontal scores in the appropriate row for the same process.

4.   Identify the importance of a process according to descending value. The higher the score the more valuable a process is from the perspective of the team members.

5.   Using the same blank matrix form to record the new prioritization of the goals, record the new prioritization of the processes on the Y-axis. (Record the value of that process in brackets or parentheses.)

H. Determine the four quadrants of the matrix.

1.   Calculate the value, or product, of each cell in the matrix by multiplying the derived value for the applicable goals by the derived value for the applicable process. (Record the product in the applicable cell.)

2.   Identify, through shading or bold lines, the top 25 per cent of cells that make up the first quadrant, thereby indicating the highest priority. (If two or more cells have the same value and could be either one quadrant or the other, place them both in the higher quadrant.)

3.   Identify, through shading or bold lines, the next 50 per cent of cells that make up the second and third quadrants. (If two or more cells have the same value and could be either one quadrant or the other, place them both in the higher quadrant.)

4.   Identify, through shading or bold lines, the lower 25 per cent of cells that make up the fourth quadrant, thereby indicating the least priority. (If two or more cells have the same value and could be either one quadrant or the other, place them both in the higher quadrant.)

Step 3: Conduct in-depth review

A. For each cell, compile and analyse data to ascertain how well the project has implemented, and is implementing, the processes for the project. Possible sources of information include:

- Budgets
- Interview notes
- Metrics
- Policies and procedures
- Project history files
- Project manual
- Schedules
- Statement of work
- Work breakdown structure

B. For each cell, determine the applicable controls, or measures of success.

1. Develop your own measures of success or extract from those in this book.
2. For each measure of success within a cell, determine how well it is implemented on the project by giving 3 points for being strong, 2 points for being moderate, and 1 point for being weak. (See Figure A1.2 for a sample.)
3. For each cell, calculate the maximum amount of possible points for that cell by counting the total number of measures of success and multiplying that number by three (for example, 20 measures of success × 3 points each = 60 points).
4. For each cell, calculate the total strong points by multiplying the number of measures of success with a value of three by three (for example, 7 strong measures of success × 3 points each = 21 points).
5. For each cell, calculate the total moderate points by multiplying the number of measures of success with a value of two by two (for example, 8 moderate measures of success × 2 = 16).
6. For each cell, calculate the total weak points by multiplying the number of measures of success with a value of one by one (for example, 5 weak measures of success × 1 point each = 5 points).
7. Add the calculated value for the strong measures to the calculated value for the moderate measures and that value to the calculated value of the weak measures to ascertain the total value for the cell (that is, 21 + 16 + 5 = 42).

8. Divide the value for the cell by the maximum amount of possible points for the cell. For example, in Figure A1.2 the value is 42/60 = 70 per cent for the 20 measures of success.
9. Use the following scale to determine the overall rating of strong, moderate, or weak for the cell and record that rating in the cell where:

100 to 75%   Strong
74 to 25%   Moderate
24 to 0%   Weak

For our example, the value of 70 per cent corresponds to a rating of moderate.

Goal Process	A	B	C
1	Moderate (70 per cent)		
2			

Fig A1.2   Sample cell

C. Select the appropriate software medium (for example, graphics, spreadsheet, word processing, or some combination) to place the matrix in final form (see Figure A1.5).

Step 4: Prepare report

A. Determine whether to prepare a written or oral report.

B. If a written report:

1. Divide the report into these five components:

   - Cover page
   - Background
   - Scope
   - Findings
   - Recommendations

2. Consider the following regarding the report:

   - Encourage review of the draft prior to publication
   - Ensure the distribution list is complete
   - Keep the report to no more than three to five pages
   - No sloppy spelling errors
   - Reference the matrix
   - Stress that this is a qualitative assessment
   - Write clearly and concisely

C. If an oral presentation:

1. Divide the report into these five components:

   - Cover page
   - Background
   - Scope
   - Findings
   - Recommendations

2. Consider the following for the presentation:

   - Arrive on time
   - Allow time for questions and answers
   - Avoid rushing into details
   - Be flexible, allow for changes
   - Distribute copies after the presentation
   - Ensure the right people have been notified
   - Stress confidentiality of findings
   - Use slides that are clear and understandable

Step 5: Conduct meeting with senior management

A. Present written or oral report.

B. Note the following:

- Absolutely no 'finger-pointing'
- Areas of improvement
- Concentrate on processes or ideas, not persons
- Present results in composite form
- Results do not guarantee project success
- Results reflect 'as is' and is not prescriptive
- Stress confidentiality of findings

C. Determine if revisions are necessary and, if so, make them and follow up.

D. Conduct another closure meeting.

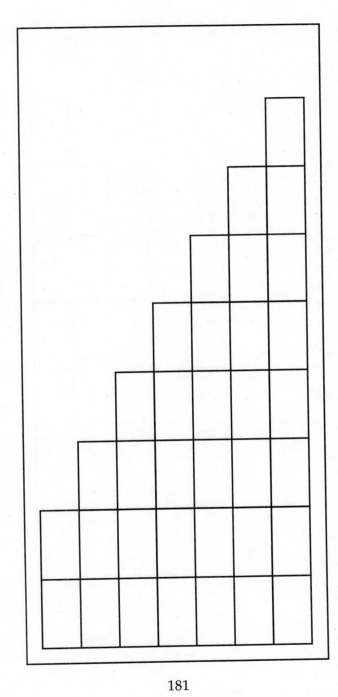

Fig A1.3 Ranking of project goals: 'step form'

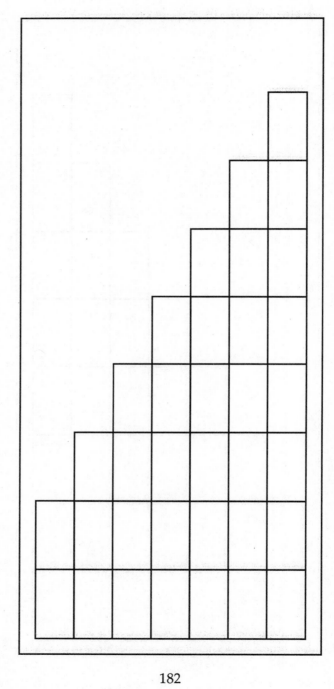

Fig A1.4 Ranking of process: 'step form'

Process / Goal				

Fig A1.5 Final project matrix

Appendix B
Software

Regardless of the technique used to perform risk identification or analysis, a wide array of tools exist to facilitate risk management.

Important insights

When selecting risk software, keep in mind the following seven parameters.

1. All software, regardless of scalability or operability, requires the overcoming of a learning curve. Users need time and assistance in understanding how to get started, to navigate through the package, and to utilize its capabilities. Unless the software package is a highly intuitive one, users will find overcoming the learning curve a difficult and slow process.
2. Define requirements. While that sounds like common sense, many project managers look at packages first and then struggle over the selection process. Such an approach wastes

time, money, and energy. It is best to determine requirements and prioritize and then select the software.

3.   Recognize that no risk tool will meet every need. Some tools
     offer only one approach (for example, the Monte Carlo tech-
     nique) while others are integrated with only one project
     management package (for example, Microsoft Project for
     Windows™).[1]

4.   Keep obsolescence protection in mind when selecting a risk
     tool. This consideration is very important when the invest-
     ment in the number and cost of tools becomes large. The
     best way to protect against obsolescence is to choose com-
     panies in the industry having a solid reputation and stabil-
     ity.

5.   Risk management and analysis software does not think. It's
     an aid for making better decisions. That is all. It will only
     provide the means and data to determine the most critical
     risks and the right controls, or measures, to establish.

6.   Finally, risk software does not guarantee a risk-free environ-
     ment. In fact, no one or nothing can do that. All that the
     software can do is to enter data and generate information to
     assist in the making of sound decisions.

7.   Output, or information, from a risk identification and analy-
     sis tool is only as good as the input, or data, fed to it. Bad
     data results in bad information. Bad information, in turn,
     results in bad decision-making.

Key features

When selecting risk identification and analysis software, project
managers isolate six factors.

1.   Determine the risk identification and analysis technique that
     the package uses. Does it support Monte Carlo simulation?
     Precedence diagramming? Decision tree analysis?

2.   Look at the statistical capabilities of the package. Does it
     provide basic statistical calculations (for example, mean,
     median, mode, and standard deviation)? Does it provide

advanced statistical calculations (for example, sampling and probability analysis)?

3. Determine how well the software integrates with other applications. Most risk identification and analysis tools support one or more project management packages. Others not only work well with project management packages but with other software, too (for example, word processing, database, spreadsheet, and graphics).

4. Look at the operating system on which the risk tool runs, noting portability, or the ability to function on different operating systems. Does the tool operate in a UNIX environment? DOS? Windows 95? Windows 3.1? Windows NT?

5. Determine the scalability, or hardware platform, the risk tool must operate on. Does it run on a mainframe? Minicomputer? Workstation? Microcomputer? Can it be used in a multi-tier (for example, client/server) environment?

6. Consider the reports and graphics the risk tool generates. Are both easy to generate? Templates to use? Clear? Concise? Meaningful?

An approach

There are many approaches to selecting risk identification and analysis software. All require a logical and methodical analysis if selection is to be efficient and effective.

Here is one such approach for selecting risk tools:

1. Define requirements
2. Prioritize each requirement
3. Analyse and score each product
4. Select top-scoring package
5. Conduct demo
6. Make a final selection
7. Train people

Step 1: Define requirements

We need to define the requirements in order to select a package that best increases productivity. The definition includes not only what the project manager needs but also what he or she wants to satisfy. Both needs and wants should incorporate current and future requirements to protect against obsolescence.

Requirements can be subdivided into three categories: technical, behavioural, and cost. Technical requirements include portability, scalability, and hardware. Behavioural requirements include user interaction issues, such as ease of use and learning curve. Cost requirements deal with available moneys.

Step 2: Prioritize each requirement

Not all requirements are equal; some are more so than others. Project managers can determine levels of importance by assigning a weight to each requirement to indicate its relative level (see Figure B1.1).

Step 3: Analyse and score each product

Project managers complete this step by collecting and reviewing information about each product and tallying the results (see Figure B1.2). This eliminates wasteful time and effort on packages that 'look nice' but do not meet requirements.

Step 4: Select top-scoring packages

Project managers might consider the top 25 per cent of the packages and review them in greater detail. The number one scoring package is not always the one to purchase. It may not be feasible because the cost of retrofitting everything may be prohibitive in time, labour, or money.

Step 5: Conduct demo

For each of the 'finalists', conduct a demo to ascertain the qualitative and quantitative features. Qualitative, or value-added, features, like user-friendliness, may not appear in the initial calculations but impact tremendously on how well users receive and use a product.

Requirements	Assigned Value
Perform decision tree analysis	2
Perform Monte Carlo simulation	2
Generate standard reports	2
Generate *ad hoc* reports	1
Generate standard graphics	2
Generate customized graphics	1
Operate in Windows environment	1
Require minimum learning curve	2
Address unit cost	1
Key: 2 = Necessary requirement 1 = Wanted, but not necessary requirement 0 = Not wanted nor necessary requirement	

Fig B1.1   How to determine requirements

Step 6: Make a final selection

Once the demo is completed, project managers have a good idea which package they want. If there is still a difficulty in choosing, then repeat steps 2 to 4 for the finalists. The latter may provide additional information to help in evaluating products.

Step 7: Train people

No matter how intuitive a product, project managers need to train people in its features and capabilities as well as teaching them how to navigate through it. Such training reduces not only

Requirements	Assigned value	Package No. 1		Package No. 2		Package No. 3	
		Value	Score	Value	Score	Value	Score
Perform decision tree analysis	2	1	2	1	2	0	0
Perform Monte Carlo simulation	2	2	4	1	2	1	2
Generate standard reports	2	1	2	0	0	1	2
Generate *ad hoc* reports	1	0	0	0	0	2	2
Generate standard graphics	2	1	2	2	4	2	4
Generate customized graphics	1	0	0	0	0	1	1
Operate in Windows environment	1	2	2	2	2	2	2
Require minimum learning curve	2	0	0	1	2	2	4
Address unit cost	1	2	2	1	1	1	1
Total score			14		13		18

Legend:
2 = Necessary requirement
1 = Wanted, but not necessary requirement
0 = Not wanted nor necessary requirement

Fig B1.2 How to select the right software

the learning curve but also levels of frustration. The aim is to enable people to use the product, not keep it on the shelf.

Overview of some popular products

Risk Master ©
Risk management software for use as a stand-alone package or with project management software like Microsoft Project© and ARTEMIS™. It uses Monte Carlo simulation to quantitatively and qualitatively analyse cost and schedule risks. *Risk Master* operates on an IBM® or compatible 386 or higher, requires 4 megabytes of memory, using PC-DOS/MS-DOS® and Windows 3.1® or higher.[2]

Q2Risk©
A Windows-based integrated qualitative and quantitative risk management system sitting on a database-independent client/server platform.[3]

in-time©
Part of a suite of software for managing projects. It provides risk control through an Earned Value Analysis report facility, graphically displaying the Budgeted Cost of Work Performed and Actual Cost of Work Performed. It supports Microsoft Project® and CA-Superproject®. *in-time* operates on a 386 or higher; requires a minimum of 1 megabyte of memory using DOS 3.1 or higher and Windows 3.0 or higher.[4]

RANK-IT®
Risk assessment software for applying the precedence diagramming method when determining and evaluating risk. It allows users to identify and rank threats, processes, and controls while applying the Delphi technique. Ranking can be based on either a weighting factor or percentage risk values. *RANK-IT* operates in a DOS/Windows environment and on IBM PC, compatibles, or PS/2 hardware with 512 KB of memory.[5]

Opera™

The name is short for Open Plan Extension for Risk Analysis. It is a risk management software package for use with Open Plan, a project management package by Welcom Software Technology. *Opera*™ enables users to define and analyse uncertainties pertaining to completion dates and cost as well as addressing earned value. *Opera*™ operates in the DOS environment and requires Open Plan and either Microsoft FoxPro® for DOS (version 2.0 or better) or Borland dBase IV® (version 1.5 or better).[6]

Monte Carlo for Primavera™

Risk analysis software for use with Primavera Project Planner, a project management package by Primavera Systems, Inc., *Monte Carlo for Primavera*™ allows users to determine the probabilities of completing a project on schedule and within budget. It also uses 'probabilistic branching' to decide the most effective action to pursue and assess the effect of a circumstance on activities. *Monte Carlo for Primavera*™ operates in the DOS, Win 3.1, Win95, or Windows NT environment and requires Primavera Project Planner.[7]

Risk+™

Risk analysis software for use with Microsoft Project for Windows, *Risk+*™ uses Monte Carlo simulation to determine probabilities of completing tasks and entire projects on schedule and within budget. This is accomplished by users entering range values for activities and costs along with probability curves to perform the Monte Carlo simulation. *Risk+*™ operates in the Win 3.1 or Win 95 environment and requires Microsoft Project for Windows.[8]

Rumor™

Risk analysis software that allows users to analyse and asses the economics and risks for projects. Users factor in costs; tangible and intangible benefits; and then calculate risks for the entire project. The software uses Monte Carlo simulation with cash flow analysis and offers a methodology and templates for economic modelling. *Rumor*™ operates in Win 3.1 environment and on Intel 486 or better hardware.[9]

@RISK

Risk analysis software for use with RISK. It enables users to preview distribution functions and assess probabilities graphically. *@RISK* covers a multitude of distribution functions (for example, extreme value or Gumbel) and creates graphics in standard spreadsheet format. The software applies Monte Carlo simulation to analyse risk data in spreadsheet packages. *@RISK* operates in a Win 3.1 and DOS environment and requires Lotus 1–2–3 for Windows or Microsoft Excel.[10]

Total Risk™

This package offers integrated risk management allowing businesses to monitor and control risk. Using their object-oriented, distributed cache technology a virtual data warehouse can be created. *Total Risk*™ operates on Windows NT and Unix.[11]

Appendix C
Common Project Management
Risks and their Implications

1 Leadership

Risk	Impacts				Possible contingency plan
	Cost	Schedule	Quality	People	
High turnover of critical team members	●	●	●	●	Conduct cross-training Assign 'back-up' team members
Indecisiveness		●		●	Restrict time available to make decisions Seek external consultant for guidance Halt project until critical decision is made
Lack of client 'buy-in'/ involvement			●	●	Encourage client review of deliverables Encourage client participation in meetings Halt project until greater involvement occurs
Lack of senior management support	●	●		●	Request review and signature of approval of project deliverables Seek out a project champion or sponsor
Lack of team consensus over project plans	●	●		●	Request greater input and review from team members Develop new project plans
Limited authority/control for project manager	●	●		●	Publish a project announcement Increase hierarchical status of the project manager
No project vision			●	●	Develop and publish a statement of work Develop and publish a vision statement
No team building			●	●	Hold frequent group meetings Encourage greater sharing of information Hold 'peer reviews' Encourage two or more people to work on the same task or deliverable
Poor communications	●	●	●	●	Hold frequent meetings Distribute documentation Develop and publish a project manual
Poor motivation of participants	●	●	●	●	Encourage greater participation in the decision-making process Assign tasks that encourage job enlargement and enrichment Assign responsibility for complete units of work

2 Definition

Risk	Impacts				Possible contingency plan
	Cost	Schedule	Quality	People	
High technological complexity	●	●	●		Seek outside consultants 'Modularize' the approach Document requirements, specifications, and design for the product Institute configuration management disciplines
Ill-defined goals and objectives			●	●	Develop or revisit statement of work Encourage client participation at meetings Establish critical milestones in the schedule
Ill-defined project scope	●	●	●		Develop or revisit statement of work Encourage client participation at meetings
Changing requirements	●	●	●	●	Revisit statement of work Establish change control
Incomplete or ill-defined requirements	●	●	●		Develop or revisit statement of work Encourage client participation at meetings Submit documents for client review and approval
Incomplete statement of work	●	●	●		Halt progress until the statement of work is complete
Unrealistic goals	●	●	●	●	Revisit the statement of work

3 Planning

Risk	Impacts				Possible contingency plan
	Cost	Schedule	Quality	People	
Inaccurate cost estimates	●				Revise work breakdown structure, resource assignments, and time estimates
Inaccurate time estimates		●			Revise work breakdown structure, resource assignments, and time estimates
Incomplete project plan	●	●	●		Review the plan with project participants, especially core team members, senior management, and client
Incomplete work breakdown structure	●	●	●		Conduct review and further refinement of the work breakdown structure
No formal estimating tools	●	●			Take money from the 'management reserve' fund to purchase tools Train people on using the tools
No historical precedence for project	●	●	●		Conduct benchmarking of projects Track and monitor project performance more closely than usual
Poor allocation of resources	●	●	●	●	Revisit project plans, focusing on resource allocation and resource levelling
Unrealistic schedules		●	●	●	Revise the statement of work, work breakdown structure, time estimates, and resource allocations Increase overtime Hire internal and external consultants

4 Organizing

Risk	Impacts				Possible contingency plan
	Cost	Schedule	Quality	People	
Inadequate communications infrastructure in place				●	Prepare and publish a project manual Establish a project library Prepare and publish an organization chart Hold frequent meetings Distribute documentation or information more widely
Lack of resources		●	●	●	Hire internal and external consultants Revise resource allocations, focusing mainly on critical path tasks
Lack of subject matter expertise	●	●	●		Hire internal and external consultants Train existing team members Cross-train team members
No documented procedures/processes			●	●	Streamline processes, thereby forcing documentation to occur Assign someone not working on critical path tasks to document procedures/processes Purchase a standardized project management methodology
Poor assignment/ allocation of tasks		●	●	●	Revise resource allocation
Too complex for resources available		●	●	●	Hire external or internal consultants with desired expertise
Wrong selection of project management software	●	●			Train people to use the tool Obtain an alternative tool by taking an organized, objective approach towards its selection Hire internal or external service with the desired tool

5 Controlling

Risk	Impacts				Possible contingency plan
	Cost	Schedule	Quality	People	
Little or no project management process in place	●	●	●	●	Purchase a project management methodology Document processes and procedures
No impact analysis of changes	●	●			Institute configuration management Institute change control
Inflexibility of project plans	●	●	●	●	Concentrate only on the critical path tasks Seek approval from client and senior management to replan
Constantly changing market conditions	●	●	●	●	Conduct periodic replanning Focus only on critical path tasks
Poor assessment of project results	●	●	●		Establish regular status and checkpoint review meetings Institute regular reporting of results
Unsatisfactory conduct of status review meetings				●	Assign new facilitator or chairperson for the meetings Have everyone collect status prior to meeting and formally present results Publish minutes of the meetings
Lack of change management	●	●	●		Establish formal change management procedures Institute configuration management
Inability to take timely corrective action	●	●	●		Establish an action item log and review at meetings Show impact to cost and schedule of delay

6 Closure

Risk	Impacts				Possible contingency plan
	Cost	Schedule	Quality	People	
Unable to capture results	●	●	●		Interview participants Conduct review of previous project activities

Incomplete winding down of activities	●	●	●	●	Replan the remaining phases of
					  the project
					Release resources gradually
					Insist on following the project
					  plan down to the last task

Glossary

Acceptable Risk
Accepting a threat if it should occur and will not stop the project; view risk as neither good nor bad but a fact of life.

Actual Cost of Work Performed (ACWP)
The amount spent to complete work up to a specific point in time.

Analysis Paralysis
Taking too long to manipulate facts and data only leads to indecisiveness.

Asch, Solomon
Conducted experiments revealing that group pressure has a substantial influence on decisions made within that group and how different ideas are acknowledged.

Assessing
The project management process for determining the environment in which a project must occur.

Behavioral Sway
Making decisions based on managerial and peer pressures.

Benchmarking
A process improvement tool for comparing and adapting processes better performed at another company.

Brainstorming
Generating ideas without any screening about a topic and listing them without criticism from anyone.

Budgeted Cost of Work Performed (BCWP)
The value of the work completed up to a specific point in time; it is also known as earned value.

Budgeted Cost of Work Scheduled (BCWS)
The cost targeted to complete if following the project plan.

Business Process Re-engineering (BPR)
Completely overhauling or replacing processes using modelling tools and workflow software.

Cassidy and Lynn
Postulated that risk infers a need for achievement.

Causal Relationship
When making a decision, know that the final results must have a relationship with that decision.

Closure
The project management process for completing the project efficiently and effectively.

Component Reuse
Using pieces or parts of a system, product, or project to solve a problem or achieve a goal.

Contingency Planning
Preparing to handle a given circumstance that may arise in the future.

Continuous Quality Improvement (CQI)
Seeks incremental change to processes by collecting data, identifying variances, receiving customer feedback, and recognizing individuals who improve processes.

Controlling
The project management process for assessing how well the project manager uses plans and organizes to meet project goals and objectives.

Death
The fifth stage of a project life cycle; when a project loses its purpose and is terminated.

Decision Trees
A risk analysis technique for describing random processes and computing the probability of a given occurrence using a tree diagram.

Decision-making
Determining the appropriate action to accomplish goals efficiently and effectively.

Decline
The fourth state of a project life cycle; when a project goes into a 'winding down' mode and begins to lose legitimacy.

Definition
The project management process for deciding in advance the goals of a project.

Delphi Approach
A technique for obtaining an independent opinion on a topic by consulting with subject matter experts.

Deming Wheel
Named after W. Edwards Deming. It consists of four processes for decision-making: plan, do, check, act.

Descriptive Model
Describes how the environment operates in an 'as is' perspective.

Earned Value
Reviewing both schedule and budget performance together by looking at three variables: Budgeted Cost for Work Scheduled (BCWS); Budgeted Cost of Work Performed (BCWP); and Actual Cost of Work Performed (ACWP).

External Risk
A threat to a project that has no control over it.

External Environment
The components outside the boundaries of a project that may directly or indirectly apply to a project, such as actors (for example, senior management), company policies, and company goals.

Feasibility
The phases of a project when a determination is made whether there is a practical alternative to current operations.

Float
The amount of time an activity can slip in the schedule before impacting the critical path.

Forced Ranking Technique
A technique whereby participants have one vote each which can be split.

Formulation
The phase of a project when the project itself defines in detail what the customer needs and wants and develops alternatives to meet those requirements.

Frequency Distributions
Collections of raw data summarized in tabular or graphical form.

Gestation
The first stage of a project life cycle that deals with the birth of a project, usually resulting in a need to be satisfied.

Growth
The second stage of a project life cycle when the project earns legitimacy and has established justification for its existence.

Herzberg, Frederick
Developed the two factor theory of motivation.

Heuristics
A risk analysis technique using a rule of thumb.

Implementation
The phase of a project when the actual building of the product occurs.

Independence
The third stage of a project life cycle; when the project becomes self-sustaining and is able to compete with other projects.

Installation
The phase of a project when the product is operational in the client's environment.

Internal Environment
The components within the boundaries of a project, such as actors (for example, project manager), procedures, goals, and the team.

Internal Risk
A threat unique to the project and caused within the project.

Janis, Irving
Developed the theory of 'groupthink', a way of thinking that occurs with extremely cohesive groups.

Leading
The project management process involving the influence of people to achieve goals and objectives.

Long-term Risk
A threat that can occur in the distant future and may have a critical impact.

Major Players
The core team, senior managers, and clients involved with a project.

Manageable Risk
A threat that project managers have some control over.

Maslow, Abraham
Developed a model for understanding human motivation.

McClelland, David
Developed the Ach, or achievement factor, for motivation.

Mean
The sum of numbers divided by the total number of items.

Measures of Success
The criteria for determining whether project deliverables meet expectations.

Median
The middle number of a group of numbers when ranked according to magnitude.

Mode
The number that occurs most frequently in a set of numbers.

Monte Carlo simulation
A risk analysis simulation that generates expected values from a random value for an appropriate probability distribution.

Non-acceptable Risk
A 'show stopper' that can halt a project.

Non-manageable Risk
Have no control over. For example, senior management arbitrarily reducing funds for the project.

Non-routine Decisions
Determining an action to take which lacks any precedent, and the results are an educated guess.

Normal Distribution
The traditional bell-shaped curve to identify control limits.

Normative, or Prescriptive, Model
A framework that describes how an environment should operate or in 'to be' perspective.

Operability
The ability to run a computer program using different operating systems. For example, Dos, Mac, Unix, Windows.

Ordinal Approach
A qualitative approach for problem solving.

Organizing
The project management process for orchestrating resources cost-effectively so as to execute project plans.

Outside Opinion
Hiring a consultant from either outside the organization or within it.

Perception
Dealing with physical and emotional appearances and relationships between the presenter and the audience prior to delivering a presentation.

Performance
Delivering a presentation.

Perspective
Analysing the presenter and the audience prior to delivering a presentation.

PERT
Program Evaluation and Review Technique. A technique to measure and control a project's progress.

Planning
The project management process for determining what steps to execute, assigning who will perform those tasks, and verifying when they must start and stop.

Portability
The ease of transfer of a computer program to different systems and environments. For example, Sun, HP, DEC.

Practice
The techniques for rehearsing a presentation.

Precedence Diagramming Method (PDM)
A risk analysis technique taking an ordinal approach to determine priorities. The prioritization reflects the ranking of variables according to some criteria to reflect importance.

Preparation
Structuring the presentation, incorporating content to support ideas, and determining the mode of delivery prior to delivering it.

Probability
Classical definitions include terms such as 'equally likely' or 'equally probable' to the ways that events can occur.

Project History Files
A historical file of documentation developed during a project.

Project Life Cycle
The flowtime of a project consisting of five simple stages: gestation, growth, independence, decline, and death.

Project Management Application Typology (PMAT)
Approach to attain an overall level of risk that an environment presents.

Project Management Methodology
A set of guidelines and instructions for leading, defining, planning, organizing, controlling, and closing projects efficiently and effectively.

Project Management
A disciplined approach towards leading, identifying, defining, planning, organizing, controlling, and closing a finite endeavour.

Project Manual
A reference book on all activities, events, schedules, financial data, and other pertinent information.

Project Phases
There are five phases: feasibility, formulation, implementation, installation, and sustaining.

Quadrant I (Dynamic Environment – Low Structure)
An environment where change occurs rapidly and administrative operations are often overlooked or viewed as a necessary evil.

Quadrant II (Dynamic Environment – High Structure)
An environment where change occurs but not as rapidly in the Low-structure Dynamic Environment. The environment is more stable and an appreciation for administrative operations is greater.

Quadrant III (Static Environment – Low Structure)
An environment where both means and ends are fairly predictable and routine; administrative operations are good 'things' to do but not that important.

Quadrant IV (Static Environment – High Structure)
An environment where change does not occur that often; the means and the ends pretty much are repeatable and lend themselves to stepwise refinement.

Risk
The occurrence of an event that has consequences, or impacts, on a project.

Risk Acceptance
When a threat arises, project managers decide to take no action.

Risk Adoption
When a threat arises, project managers coexist with it.

Risk Analysis
The second step of risk management. It involves analysing by converting collected data using a selected technique during risk identification.

Risk Aversion
Risk management is predicated on the worst-case scenarios while simultaneously trying to address all risk situations.

Risk Avoidance
Project managers take action to avoid one or more threats.

Risk Control
The third step of risk management. It involves identifying the measures, or controls, to lessen or avoid the impact of a threat on a process or component.

Risk Exposure
The impact of a threat on a product, system, or project.

Risk Identification
The first step of risk management, considerable effort occurs to identify and rank the major processes, or components, of a project; its major goals; and the relative importance of each one *vis-à-vis* others.

Risk Perception
How people perceive threats.

Risk Pro-action
Ensuring that the appropriate project management processes are in place to handle threats efficiently and effectively.

Risk Reporting
The fourth step of risk management; once the identification, analysis, and control identifications are complete, this step occurs, either as a formal presentation or document.

Risk Transfer
Project managers share the impact of threats with another entity, such as with another project or a consultant.

Routine Decisions
Determining action to take that will have predictable results, based upon some standard operating procedure.

Scalability
Ability to run a computer program on different machine types. For example, mainframes, desktops, minicomputer systems.

Scientific Method
A technique that forces objectivity when performing risk management involving defining, analysing, developing, and testing hypotheses.

Scribe
The person who takes the notes during the session on building a risk matrix.

Short-term Risk
A threat that can have an immediate impact and its effect may be critical.

Skinner, B.F.
Developed a model of human behaviour that can help determine one's perception of risk and the results of risk management.

Standard Deviation
A value that measures dispersion about the mean.

Statement of Work
A signed agreement identifying vision, mission, goals, objectives, and responsibilities of a project.

Stochastic Processes
Occurrences with a finite number of outcomes and given probabilities.

Structural Functional
A perspective recognizing that each component in a system plays a role, albeit some more important than others.

Subject Matter Experts
The most knowledgeable people on a project.

Sustaining
The phase of a project when the client has direct control over the product.

Three-point Estimate
The use of three variables to estimate the time to complete a task. The three variables are optimistic, pessimistic, and most likely.

Variation
The spread of data about an average value.

Venn Diagrams
An algebraic depiction of events in graphic form.

Vroom, Victor
Developed a model on how the goals of individuals influence their behaviour along with the probability that their behaviour will lead to goal achievement.

Work Breakdown Structure
A detailed listing of tasks to complete the project.

Recommended Reading

Cooper, Dale., and Chapman, C. B. *Risk Analysis for Large Projects: Models, Methods, and Cases.* New York, NY: John Wiley and Sons, 1987.

de Newfrille, Richard. *Applied Systems Analysis.* New York, NY: McGraw-Hill, 1990.

Donnelly, James H., Jr., Gibson, James L., and Ivancevich, John M. *Fundamentals of Management, 4th ed.* Homewood, Ill.: Business Publications, Inc., 1981.

Drucker, Peter. *Managing for Results.* New York, NY: Harper and Row Publishers, 1964.

—— *Management.* New York, NY: Harper Colophon Books, 1985.

Fallon, William (ed.). *AMA Management Handbook, 2nd ed.* New York, NY: AMACOM, 1983.

Fitzgerald, Jerry, and Fitzgerald, Arda. *Fundamentals of Systems Analysis.* New York, NY: John Wiley and Sons, 1987.

—— *Designing Controls into Computerized Systems.* Redwood City, CA: Jerry FitzGerald & Associates, 1990.

Garfield, Charles. *Peak Performers.* New York, NY: William Morrow and Co., 1986.

Guideline for Automatic Data Processing Risk Analysis. FIPS Pub 65. 1 August 1979.

Guide to Auditing for Controls and Security: A Systems Development Life Cycle Approach. US Dept of Commerce #500–153. April 1988.

Janis, Irving L. *Victims of Groupthink.* New York, NY: Houghton Mifflin Co., 1972.

Keirsey, David, and Bates, Marilyn. *Please Understand Me.* Del Mar, CA: Prometheus Nemesis Book Company, 1984.

Kepner, Charles H., and Tregoe, Benjamin B. *The Rational Manager.* New York, NY: McGraw-Hill, 1965.

Kerzner, Harold. *Project Management, 2nd ed.* New York, NY: Van Nostrand Reinhold Co., 1984.

Kliem, Ralph L., and Ludin, Irwin S. *Data Processing Manager's Model Reports and Formats.* Englewood Cliffs, NJ: Prentice Hall, 1992.

—— *The Noah Project.* Aldershot: Gower, 1993.

—— *The People Side of Project Management.* Aldershot: Gower, 1992.

—— *Stand and Deliver.* Aldershot: Gower, 1995.

—— *Just-in-Time Systems for Computing Environments.* Westport, CT: Quorum Books, 1994.

Moody, Paul E. *Decision Making.* New York, NY: McGraw-Hill, 1983.

Moore, Peter G. *The Business of Risk.* London: Cambridge University Press, 1986.

Posner, Mitchell J. *Executive Essentials: The Complete Sourcebook for Success.* New York, NY: Avon, 1987.

Russo, J. Edward, and Schoemaker, Paul H. *Decision Traps.* New York, NY: Simon and Schuster, 1989.

Weston, J. Fred, and Brigham, Eugene F. *Managerial Finance* (6th edn), Hinsdale, Ill.: The Dryden Press, 1978.

Whitten, Neal. *Managing Software Development Projects.* New York, NY: John Wiley and Sons, 1990.

Notes

Preface

1. *Computerworld*, 11 April 1994, p. 118.
2. Standish Group International Inc., *Application Development Trends*, January 1995, pp. 41–3.
3. *Network World*, 12 September 1994, p. 55.
4. *Computerworld*, 13 June 1994, p. 1.
5. *Newsweek*, 15 May 1995, pp. 64–5.

1 An Overview

1. W. Edwards Deming, *The New Economy for Industry, Government, Education*, Cambridge, Mass.: MIT Center for Advanced Engineering Study, 1993.

2 Project Risks: Origins and Impacts

1. Ralph L. Kliem and Irwin S. Ludin, *The People Side of Project Management*, Aldershot: Gower, 1992.
2. Ibid.
3. Ibid.
4. Ibid., especially Chapter 3.

3 The Psychology of Risk Management

1. Abraham Maslow in Donnelly, J.H., Gibson, J.L. and Ivancevich, J.M., *Fundamentals of Management*, 4th edn, Plano, TX: Business Publications Inc., 1981, pp 220–222.
2. Frederick Herzberg in Donnelly, J.H., Gibson, J.L. and Ivancevich, J.M., *Fundamentals of Management*, 4th edn, Plano, TX: Business Publications Inc., 1981, pp 228–232.
3. David McClelland in Drucker, P.F., *Management: Tasks, Responsibilities, Practices*, New York: Harper and Row, 1985, p. 234.
4. Cassidy, T. and Lynn, R. 'A multi-dimensional approach to achievement motivation: the development of a comprehensive measure', *Journal of Occupational Psychology*, Vol. 62 (1989), pp. 301–12.
5. Ibid.
6. Victor Vroom in Donnelly, J.H., Gibson, J.L. and Ivancevich, J.M., *Fundamentals of Management*, 4th edn, Plano, TX: Business Publications Inc., 1981, pp 231–232.
7. B.F. Skinner in Donnelly, J.H., Gibson, J.L. and Ivancevich, J.M., *Fundamentals of Management*, 4th edn, Plano TX: Business Publications Inc., 1981, pp. 242–244.
8. Irving Janis, *Victims of Groupthink*, Boston, Mass.: Houghton Mifflin Co., 1972.
9. Solomon Asch in Donnelly, J.H., Gibson, J.L. and Ivancevich, J.M., *Fundamentals of Management*, 4th edn, Plano, TX: Business Publications Inc., 1981, p. 268.

5 Step One: Risk Identification

1. B.H. West, E.N. Griesbach, J.D. Taylor and L. Taylor, *Prentice Hall Encyclopedia of Mathematics*, Englewood Cliffs, NJ: Prentice Hall, 1982.

6 Step Two: Risk Analysis

1. For a discussion of just-in-time environments and cultivation of long-term customer–supplier relationships, see Ralph L. Kliem and Irwin S. Ludin, *Just-In-Time Systems for Computing Environments*, Westport, CT: Quorum Books, 1994.
2. Not to be confused with precedence diagramming for network scheduling. For an in-depth description of PDM see Part III, the case study of the RAW project.

7 Step Three: Risk Control

1. Ralph L. Kliem and Irwin S. Ludin, *Just-In-Time Systems for Computing Environments*, Westport, CT: Quorum Books, 1994.
2. Ibid.

8 Step Four: Risk Reporting

1. Ralph. L. Kliem and Irwin S. Ludin, *Data Processing Manager's Model Reports and Formats*, Englewood Cliffs, NJ: Prentice Hall, 1992.
2. Ralph L. Kliem and Irwin S. Ludin, *Stand and Deliver: The Fine Art of Presentation*, Aldershot: Gower, 1995. In this business novel the authors show how David Michaels learns about effective presentation.
3. Ibid.

9 A Case Study

1. Ralph L. Kliem and Irwin S. Ludin, *The Noah Project: The Secrets of Practical Project Management*, Aldershot: Gower, 1994.
2. Ralph L. Kliem and Irwin S. Ludin, *Stand and Deliver: The Fine Art of Presentation*, Aldershot: Gower, 1995.

Appendix B: Software

1. Microsoft Project for Windows™ is a product of the Microsoft Corporation. Microsoft Corporation, One Microsoft Way, Redmund, WA 98052–6399 USA. Telephone: (303) 684 0914.
2. For more information on *Risk Master©*, contact: Planning and Consultancy Service, Unit 6, Hynesbury Road, Christchurch, Dorset BH23 4ER. Telephone: 01202 490559.
3. Ibid., for *Q2Risk*.
4. For more information on *in-time©*, contact: The Projects Group plc, 1 Mulgrave Road, Sutton, Surrey SM2 6LE. Telephone: 0181–770–9393.
5. For more information on *RANK-IT®* contact: Jerry Fitzgerald & Associates, 506 Barkentine Lane, Redwood City, California, USA. Telephone: (415) 591–5676.
6. At the time of writing, a Win 3.1 and Win95 version called Open Plan Professional™ which includes risk software is planned to be on the market. For more information, contact: Welcome Software Technology, 15995 N., Barkers's Landing, Suite 275, Houston, Texas 77079–2494, USA. Telephone: (713) 558–0514.
7. For more information on *Monte Carlo for Primavera™* contact: Primavera Systems Inc., Two Bala Plaza, Bala Cynwyd, Pennsylvania 19004–1586, USA. Telephone: (610) 667–8600.
8. For more information on *Risk+™* contact: Program Management Solutions Inc., 553 N. Pacific Coast Highway, Suite B–177, Redondo Beach, California 90278, USA. Telephone: (805) 898–9571.

9. For more information on *Rumor*™ contact: D.M. Witte and Associates Inc., PO Box 260145, Plano, Texas 75026, USA. Telephone: (214) 964–7602.
10. For more information on *@Risk* contact: Palisade Corporation, 31 Decker Road, Newfield, New York 14867, USA. Telephone: (607) 277–8000.
11. For more information on *Total Risk*™ contact: Redpoint Software Inc., One Cabot Road, Suite 190, Hudson, Massachusetts 01749, USA. Telephone: (508) 567–0801.

Index

Advanced Project Management

A Structured Approach

Third Edition

F L Harrison

When this book first appeared in 1981 it quickly acquired a reputation for excellence on both sides of the Atlantic. For this third edition the text has been radically revised and the author presents a new approach designed to be used as a framework for the total integration of project management work. According to Mr Harrison, the elements that determine the success or failure or a project are:

- The structure of the project organization
- The methodology used for planning and control
- How human relations problems and conflicts are handled
- The effectiveness of integration.

The author deals in depth with all these topics.

This is a book that successfully bridges the gap between introductory texts on project management and specialist works on professional practice. Its aim is twofold: to provide both a guide for managers, engineers, accountants and others involved in project work and a textbook for advanced students of project and construction management.

Gower

The Essentials of Project Management

Dennis Lock

Project management skills are no longer just required by project managers, but by most of us in the natural course of our working lives. *The Essentials of Project Management* is a practical primer drawn from Dennis Lock's comprehensive and highly regarded textbook *Project Management*, which is now in its Sixth Edition and has sold tens of thousands of copies. In order to specifically answer the needs of the non-specialist, the content has been carefully selected and organized to form an accessible introduction to the subject.

The result is a concise but well-rounded account of project management techniques, concentrating on the key tasks of project definition, organization, estimating, planning and control, and paying special attention to the role of purchasing. With the aid of examples and illustrations, the book describes the essential project management procedures and explains how and when they should be used.

This is an ideal introduction for anyone for whom project management is part of their professional role (or who would like it to be), or for students for whom it is a component within a broader course.

Gower

Gower Handbook of Management Skills

Third Edition

Edited by Dorothy M Stewart

'This is the book I wish I'd had in my desk drawer when I was first a manager. When you need the information, you'll find a chapter to help; no fancy models or useless theories. This is a practical book for real managers, aimed at helping you manage more effectively in the real world of business today. You'll find enough background information, but no overwhelming detail. This is material you can trust. It is tried and tested.'

So writes Dorothy Stewart, describing in the preface the unifying theme behind the new edition of this bestselling *Handbook*. This puts at your disposal the expertise of 25 specialists, each a recognized authority in their particular field. Together, this adds up to an impressive 'one stop library' for the manager determined to make a mark.

Chapters are organised within three parts: Managing Yourself, Managing Other People, and Managing Business. Part 1 deals with personal skills and includes chapters on self-development and information technology. Part 2 covers people skills such as listening, influencing and communication. Part 3 looks at finance, project management, decision-making, negotiating and creativity. A total of 12 chapters are completely new to this edition, and the rest have been rigorously updated to fully reflect the rapidly changing world in which we work.

Each chapter focuses on detailed practical guidance, and ends with a checklist of key points and suggestions for further reading.

Gower

Gower Handbook of Project Management

Second Edition

Edited by Dennis Lock

The first edition of this handbook was published in 1987 under the title *Project Management Handbook*. With its uniquely authoritative and comprehensive coverage of the subject, it quickly established itself as the standard work.

For this new edition the text has been revised and updated throughout to reflect recent developments. Eight entirely new chapters have been added dealing with such diverse topics as the impact of the European Community, project investment appraisal and environmental responsibility. More than twenty individuals and organizations have pooled their knowledge and experience to produce a practical treatment which ranges from first principles to some of the most advanced techniques now in use.

It is difficult to imagine anyone concerned with industrial or commercial projects who would not profit from a study of this *Handbook.*

Gower

The Management Skills Book

Conor Hannaway and Gabriel Hunt

There is virtually no limit to the skills a manager is expected to use. Some are required every day, others once a month or even once a year. From managing employee performance to chairing meetings, from interviewing staff to making retirement presentations, the list seems endless. How can managers be effective in all these areas? How can they know what to do in every situation?

The Management Skills Book is designed to help all managers facing the challenge of constant change. It is an easy-to-access practical reference work setting out in more than 100 brief guides the elements of the skills needed to succeed as a manager. Each guide is presented in a clear point-by-point style enabling the reader to absorb the key ideas without having to work through a tangle of theory. New and experienced managers alike will welcome the book as a powerful aid to increased effectiveness.

Gower

The New Unblocked Manager

A Practical Guide to Self-Development

Dave Francis and Mike Woodcock

This is unashamedly a self-help book, written for managers and supervisors who wish to improve their effectiveness. In the course of their work with thousands of managers over a long period the authors have discovered twelve potential 'blockages' that stand in the way of managerial competence. They include, for example, negative personal values, low creativity and unclear goals.

By means of a self-evaluation exercise, the reader first identifies the blockages most significant to them. There follows a detailed explanation of each blockage and ideas and materials for tackling the problem.

This is a heavily revised edition of a book that, under its original title, *The Unblocked Manager*, was used by many thousands of managers around the world and appeared in ten languages. The new edition reflects the changed world of management and owes much to the feedback supplied by practising managers.

In its enhanced form the book will continue to provide a comprehensive framework for self-directed development.

Gower

The Noah Project

The Secrets of Practical Project Management

Ralph L Kliem and Irwin S Ludin

A Gower Novel

This book is a novelization of project management. The characters and events are fictitious; however the techniques, tools, and circumstances described in each chapter are real for just about every project in any environment, from technical to financial. The scenes explain project management from the vantage point of David Michaels, a young executive working for a private zoo. He must manage the dismantling of the zoo through to a successful conclusion. He has little idea how to go about such a task until he meets Noah...

David encounters common pitfalls such as failure to achieve targets on time, budgeting restrictions, an already unreasonable schedule cut back even further, and of course the inevitable staff conflict. In his moments of crisis Noah forces David to think for himself, thereby encouraging the reader to do the same.

The authors have chosen the setting intentionally to show how anyone in any organization can put the methods and concepts of project management to use. The book also includes a 'model' project manual which can be adapted easily to the reader's own projects. Anyone looking for an enjoyable introduction to the secrets of project management will find it in *The Noah Project.*

Gower

Project Leadership

Second Edition

Wendy Briner, Colin Hastings and Michael Geddes

The bestselling first edition of this book broke new ground by focusing on the leadership aspects of project management rather than the technical. This radically revised edition is substantially reorganized, to introduce much new material and experience and bring the applications up to date.

Project leaders now exist in many different types of organizations, and they and their projects extend far wider than the construction work where traditional project management began. This new edition begins by explaining why the project way of working has been so widely and enthusiastically adopted, and provides new material on the role and key competences of project leaders in a wide range of different organizations. The authors provide invaluable guidance to senior managers struggling to create the context within which project work can thrive as well as be controlled. A new section, 'Preparing the Ground' reflects their increased emphasis on getting projects off to the right start, with new insights into the scoping process designed to ensure all parties agree on objectives. It also demonstrates the importance of understanding the organizational and political factors involved if the project is to succeed in business terms. Part III shows how to handle the issues that arise at each stage of the project's life including a whole new section on the critical process of project team start up. The final section contains a thought-provoking 'action summary' and a guide to further sources of information and development.

Project leadership and the project way of working has moved on. This book will provide both a conceptual framework and a set of practical tools for all those who find themselves permanently or occasionally in the project leader role, as well as an invaluable guide to setting up and maintaining project activity.

Gower

Project Management

Sixth Edition

Dennis Lock

Dennis Lock's bestselling book covers the project management process from initial appraisal to closedown, using methods that range from simple charts to powerful computer systems. The relevant techniques can be applied with profit whether the project is worth £1000 or £100m. Every aspect is explained in detail with the aid of illustrations and examples. The projects described are drawn from many different industries, so that the book will appeal to the widest possible range of readers.

For this sixth edition the text has been thoroughly revised and extended to reflect current practices and technology. New case studies have been added, all the computer examples have been reworked and there is increased emphasis on the precedence system of networking. This is a book that will continue to be the standard work on the subject for managers and students alike.

Features new to the Sixth Edition:

- Larger format and reader-friendly page design
- Text is considerably reworked and extended
- Many new case studies

Gower